D1707053

30 DAYS IN EXILE

Living for Christ with Courage and Expectancy in the West

ROGER SAPPINGTON

CENTRALPRESS
Ministry Resources from
Central Bible Church

Published by Central Press
Central Bible Church
8001 Anderson Boulevard
Fort Worth, Texas 76120
www.wearecentral.org

First Printing 2021

To my partner in exile, Kelly,
and our children, Colin, Brady, and Harper.

Also to my "brothers and sisters" at Central Bible Church.

May the Lord lead us to be gracious followers of Jesus,
who are faithful and hopeful in these days.

THE JOURNEY

Introduction
LIFE IN OZ

I N THE 1939 CLASSIC MOVIE *The Wizard of Oz*, Dorothy finds her-self transported via a Kansan twister to the magical, technicol-or land of Oz – a place full of wonder, yellow brick, merriment, and the occasional wicked witch. Dorothy's experience in Oz, though at times frightening, is generally filled with the joys of friendship and hope. In 1984, when Walt Disney Pictures decid-ed to produce a sequel to the much-loved children's fantasy, the Oz it constructed was far darker and more sinister. Hope gave way to oppression. Companionship was impersonal and de-tached. *The Return to Oz* presented a bleak place no child would ever want to visit.

Today, many Christians in America feel as though they have been dropped via a cultural tornado into some strange, chaotic Oz. The place they call home just doesn't feel familiar anymore. In fact, it feels almost foreign. Like exiles taken to an unfamiliar and hostile nation, American Christians sense that they are now aliens in this place. Truth is now subjective or irrelevant. Sexual ethics are Corinthian at best. Civility and decorum in broader public life (and especially in electoral politics) have been thrown by the wayside. Racial tensions appear to be continually on the rise. Religious liberty is in jeopardy.

Though many would like to find a pair of ruby red slippers to make their way back to a more comfortable place, that is im-possible. The cultural and religious shifts evident in our nation have been slowly but steadily forming over the course of decades. There will be no quick return to Christian influence in American culture and society. In fact, we need to accept the reality that America will never be anything like what people envision it was in the 1950s or 1980s. Those two decades of the second half of the twentieth century most represent the ideal for many conservative, Christian Americans. They were periods of simultaneous economic expansion, national unity, and church growth.

However, ultimately, both of those decades led to seasons of disillusionment in the years that followed, especially among young people. The reason being: in neither of those decades did deep, authentic spiritual awakening occur in America. Though churches were growing in both periods, so was consumerism. In the 1950s racism was endemic and injustice was commonplace. As the Cold War continued, the 1980s fostered an uncritical nationalism among many Americans that led some Christians to increasingly place country before God in their allegiances.

"Kansas" was never as utopic as we remember it. That is not to say that one period may not have been more influenced by Christianity than another, it is simply to point out that in every era since the rebellion in the Garden, idolatry of some kind has held sway over every culture and every nation. This is why the New Testament regularly uses the metaphor of exile to describe the experience of God's people. This place was never meant to be our home or feel like our home. As the writer of Hebrews wrote of the great men and women of the faith, "they acknowledged that they were strangers and exiles on the earth" (Hebrews 11:13). This world was foreign and unfamiliar to them. The word "exile" in the Greek means *resident alien* – a person who lives in one nation but holds citizenship elsewhere. And that is true of every Christian; though we happen to live in some nation on earth, our citizenship is in the kingdom of heaven (Philippians 3:20). As Christians in America, we have always been resident aliens. It is just that in recent days that fact has become more and more clear.

I know many of you feel discouraged by what you see happening within our culture and how that is affecting people in our churches. Though I, too, am concerned by what I see, I am also hopeful because the Lord continues to remind me of two things. First, he has been bringing to memory some of the historical periods of the Church that were also characterized by hostility from the broader culture. The first three centuries of the Church in the Roman Empire were absolutely representative of this. During that time, the Lord not only sustained his people, but "grew their number and, ultimately, their influence." Second, the Lord continues to point me to truth from Scripture that settles my anxious heart. Maybe Jesus' words to Peter are most relevant: "*on this rock I will build my church, and the gates of hell shall not prevail against it*" (Matthew 16:18). Regardless of how bad things get, the Church will not only endure, but will prevail.

I have written *30 Days in Exile: Living for Christ with Courage and Expectancy in the West* with the hope that after spending a month studying some key texts of Scripture you will have greater clarity in your calling as a Christian exile and deeper encouragement to live faithfully for Christ. May the Lord use this devotional study to strengthen your witness and intensify your love for Jesus and your neighbors.

On the journey with you,
Roger Sappington

Thus, says the LORD of hosts, the God of Israel, to all the exiles whom I have sent into exile from Jerusalem to Babylon.

Jeremiah 29:4

When you go through a trial, the sovereignty of God is the pillow upon which you lay your head.

Charles Spurgeon

1

IN THE DRIVER'S SEAT

LIFE THROWS US CURVEBALLS. Situations arise that take us off our desired course, leading us down treacherous paths or veering us through muddy avenues. As we make our way through these trials, our trust in God is sure to be tested. The Enemy often seizes these opportunities to whisper one of two questions in our ear: 1) Does God really have your best in mind? and, 2) Is God actually in control of your journey? Questioning God's goodness and sovereignty has been the devil's tactic from the very beginning. Since the Garden, he has been luring God's image-bearers into deserts of doubt, where they might reject their Creator's sovereign goodness.

In 597 B.C. some 3,000 Jews had their lives turned upside down when they were forcibly removed from their homes in Jerusalem and brought into exile in Babylon. Though most of these exiles were not severely mistreated in their new confines, life would never be the same for them. They were now foreigners in the land of their enemies. These exiles spoke a different language, had an exclusive religion, and followed strange customs. Without doubt they would have been treated with disdain by the Babylonian natives. Beyond being outsiders, these Jews had also been stripped of the key physical aspects of God's covenantal favor toward Israel – the land, the Temple, and the Davidic kingship.

Knowing the exiles' situation was sure to lead them to question God's sovereign goodness, the prophet Jeremiah penned a letter to encourage them. Jeremiah opens his letter with these words: *"Thus, says the LORD of hosts, the God of Israel, to all the exiles whom I have sent into exile"* (Jeremiah 29:4). The Lord's first words through his prophet to this beleaguered group were meant to instill a measure of confidence. God declared that he, not Nebuchadnezzar, was ultimately responsible for the exiles' condition and location. He had been in control the whole time. Nebuchadnezzar was simply a means to bring about Yahweh's desired end.

As we read the words of verse 4 declaring God's sovereignty over the Jews' exile, we might ask, "If God had good intentions for his people, why would he allow this to happen?" This is a not a bad question and, in some respects, demands an answer. First, it is important to note that the Jewish people had been warned time and again that continual disobedience would bring about God's judgment through captivity in another nation (Deuteronomy 28:15-68; Jeremiah 25:1-14). Second, even though some portion of the exiles' plight was in connection to God's punishment, he still cared for his people and had divine purposes for them. The NIV's translation of Jeremiah 29:4 sheds some light on Yahweh's concern for the exiles. Instead of rendering the verse, "I have *sent* you," the NIV translates it, "I have *carried* you." Though both senses are found in the original language, the latter puts the emphasis on the intentional activity of a caring Father. As we consider our own "exile" in this world, it is important for us to see our condition through the same lens – God's sovereign care of us.

Though we have not been forcibly removed from our homes and brought to some strange city, Christians in the West have increasingly become "foreigners" in a culture that once felt more like home. In this cultural dislocation and loss of influence, many want to pass blame on certain political, cultural, and generational forces. Some blame the Liberals; others blame the Conservatives. Some blame the Millennials; others blame the Boomers. However, it is important to note that our state as Christian exiles is not primarily based on how much we feel separate from the culture, but rather it is a spiritual reality that our true home and identity are in heaven, not on earth. Though this is the case, it is also true that the more hostile a society is toward the Christian faith, the more Christians in that space realize their exilic condition.

As we consider our experience of both spiritual and cultural exile in the West, we would do well to remember that as in the case of the Jewish exile to Babylon, the Lord is using human means to accomplish his divine purposes. We need to accept that God has allowed these cultural circumstances to take place to reset our course so that we may know him more deeply and be more faithful as his representatives in this land. He has not abandoned the American church; he will never do that. Instead of being consumed with how to "return" to a cultural location that feels more like "home," let us listen to God's Word for how to be his ambassadors in this time and place.

PRAYER

Father, I trust you; you are in control of my life. Like the shepherd in Psalm 23, you lead me to "green pastures" and "still waters," but you also lead me through dangerous valleys. You are with me all the way, providing guidance and protection. Help me to trust you in this time and place in which I find myself. May I live in light of your sovereign goodness that has carried me here. Amen.

PONDER

1. Does it give you comfort knowing God was the one chiefly responsible for the Jews' exile to Babylon? Why or why not?
2. How have you seen God "carry" you into and through difficult seasons?
3. What part of the American experience today makes you most feel like a Christian exile?

Build houses and live in them; plant gardens
and eat their produce. Take wives and have
sons and daughters; take wives for your sons,
and give your daughters in marriage,
that they may bear sons and daughters;
multiply there, and do not decrease.

Jeremiah 29:5-6

And God blessed them. And God said
to them, "Be fruitful and multiply and fill
the earth and subdue it, and have dominion
over the fish of the sea and over the birds
of the heavens and over every living thing
that moves on the earth."

Genesis 1:28

2

BE FRUITFUL AND MULTIPLY

A S THE JEWISH EXILES' TIME IN BABYLON grew from weeks to months, many must have experienced bouts of depression. There would be no immediate rescue; no quick return home. Most were simply surviving from one day to the next. Trauma has a way of numbing the senses and reducing one's ability to foster a disposition of hope. To say it another way, the exiles were most likely in a pitiable state. Then came Jeremiah's letter with a wildly different tone. Build. Plant. Marry. Increase. Multiply. Despite their fear, anger and dejection, God was calling his people in exile to flourish.

In some ways, Yahweh was telling this group of displaced Jews to live in Babylon as they had lived in Judah. They were to carry out life as normal – marrying and having children, carrying out domestic and economic activity, building lives and communities. Yet, in Babylon, the way they did life together and how they lived among their Babylonian neighbors would speak volumes about the nature of the God they worshipped. Yahweh desired that they live out in the open among their captors. They couldn't shine as lights in dark places if they were hidden away.

For these exiles, God was also calling them to a kind of new beginning. The words of Jeremiah 29:5-6 are an echo of the Creator's mandate to the first human family – "*Be fruitful and multiply and fill the earth and subdue it*" (Genesis 1:28). As God's image-bearers, Adam and Eve were to increase across the earth, bringing it into subjection to the Creator's compassionate reign. Yahweh had given them representative rule to extend his kingdom on earth and to worship him through the agency of their calling. Unfortunately, Adam and Eve relinquished these roles when they chose to side with the serpent and rebel against their King. Their decision had grave consequences: sin entered this sacred space and brokenness was the banner over an earthly kingdom that was now under the sway of the serpent.

Generations later, however, God would break through the clouds of despair and appoint one of the earth dwellers as the new ambassador of his kingdom. Abraham would be blessed through his fellowship with Yahweh and would be called to extend God's blessing to every family on the earth (Genesis 12:1-3). God would also promise him that his descendants would be as numerous *"as the stars of heaven and as the sand that is on the seashore"* (Genesis 22:17). Abraham's family would be fruitful and multiply—in Egypt and in Canaan. Now, here in Babylon, these descendants of Abraham were being told to *"multiply there, and do not decrease"* (29:6). Their location had changed but their mission had not. They were to be a growing community of worshippers whose lives honored the God of Abraham, Isaac, and Jacob.

Our calling and identity as Christians have continuity with Abraham and his descendants. Not only are we Abraham's children by faith (Galatians 3:7-9), but through the Great Commission's gospel mandate, the Lord is fulfilling his promise that through Abraham all the nations of the earth will be blessed (Matthew 28:19-20). So, even while living in a Western culture that grows increasingly hostile to the Christian faith, we should seek to "increase" and "multiply." That increase and multiplication ought to be pursued in so many different ways, but I want to share a few ideas:

1. Share the gospel broadly among your neighbors, coworkers, peers, etc.
2. Disciple all generations with intentionality – children, students, and adults.

3. Plant new small groups and churches.
4. Encourage Christian families to have many children and disciple them well.
5. Grow the number of Christ-centered schools and businesses.
6. Enter into spaces where there is a void of any Christian presence.
7. Advocate and act on behalf of the vulnerable and those who are oppressed.
8. Fund Bible translation projects around the world.

PRAYER

Lord, from the very beginning you have called us to be fruitful and multiply. That calling has continued in every era and location where your people have been. Even when the Jews were in exile in a foreign land, you called them to flourish. You wanted them to increase in their influence and grow as a people so your glory would be made known to their Babylonian neighbors. If that was your calling for them, then surely you have called us as your Spirit-filled Body to live fruitfully in our day. Help us to do so. Amen.

PONDER

1. What do you make of the fact that God called the Jews to "multiply" even under the difficulties of exile?
2. What are some ways you feel overwhelmed by the challenges that Christians face (and could face) in our culture?
3. How might God be leading you to "increase" your Christian influence in exile?

But seek the welfare of the city where
I have sent you into exile, and pray to
the LORD on its behalf, for in its welfare
you will find your welfare.

Jeremiah 29:7

The Bible tells us to love our neighbors, and
also to love our enemies; probably because
they are generally the same people.

G. K. Chesterton

3

WELFARE WORKERS

M ANY CHRISTIANS TODAY ARE WONDERING what posture they should have toward a culture and society that is increasingly rejecting biblical values. Should they continue to lovingly engage? Should they willfully resist? Or, would strategically withdrawing be the best way forward? Though at different times and in different ways each of these options may be the right one to employ, the Lord gave the exiles in Babylon an answer that might surprise you. Jeremiah wrote, *"But seek the welfare of the city where I have sent you into exile, and pray to the LORD on its behalf, for in its welfare you will find your welfare"* (Jeremiah 29:7). They weren't to physically resist. They weren't to run and hide. Yahweh was calling them to love and serve their captors and pray for the Babylonians to know God's glory and goodness. The Jewish exiles were to be active and intentional in bringing God's blessings to their Babylonian neighbors.

The word translated "welfare" in verse 7 is the Hebrew word "shalom." Though it does mean "peace," it is far richer than simply referring to the cessation of conflict. It is better understood as "wholeness" or "prosperity," or even "flourishing." The exiles were to pursue the very best for the citizens of Babylon. They would do this by the ways they worked under the authority of their bosses. By using their various gifts and abilities to bring order and beauty to society. In how they responded to the decrees of the government (so long as those decrees were in keeping with their faith). By the ways they served those who were vulnerable – widows, orphans, the poor, the sojourner. By showing care and generosity to neighbors through famine, sickness, and war. And, finally, they could seek the welfare of the Babylonians by pointing them to their God.

Yahweh had missional purposes for his people, but to be faithful to this call they were going to need to change their posture toward those they most likely hated. They were going to need to go from "arms crossed" to "arms open." This would not be easy. It is not our default position to love those who threaten our way of living, but this is the way of our God who shows compassion on his enemies, who even blesses those who hate him (Luke 6:35).

Many of us in the West need to consider a change of posture toward our culture as well. Our fear and disgust have often led to anger or resentment. In our anger we have not loved others as Christ has loved us. In an article for Ligonier Ministries entitled, "Christian Exiles," John Piper shares a better approach:

> The fact that we are exiles on the earth does not mean that we don't care what becomes of culture. Rather, it means that we exert our influence as happy, yet brokenhearted outsiders. Our joy is a brokenhearted joy because human culture — in every society — dishonors Christ, glories in its shame, and is bent on self-destruction. However, we do not smirk at the misery or the merrymaking of immoral culture. We weep. Or we should. This is my main point: being exiles does not mean being cynical. It does not mean being indifferent or uninvolved. The salt of the earth does not mock rotting meat. Where it can, it saves and seasons. Where it can't, it weeps. And the light of the world does not withdraw, saying 'good riddance' to godless darkness. It labors to illuminate.

May we work to bring the light of Christ to our communities and nation! As Bruce Springsteen once sang, "You can't start a fire worrying about your little world falling apart." If we are so focused on what we have lost culturally or so angrily obsessed with how to reclaim it, then we are not going to start a gospel fire in this day.

Jeremiah concludes verse 7 with the words—*"for in [Babylon's] welfare you will find your welfare."* I wonder if part of the reason the Church finds itself in its current position in the United States is because we have been a little too busy fighting culture wars instead of seeking the blessing of our nation. This is not to say that Christians shouldn't stand for truth and justice in the public square. However, it is to ask whether our primary posture has been "arms crossed" or "arms open."

PRAYER

Jesus, I want to start a gospel fire by seeking the welfare of the community and nation in which I live. Help me to love my neighbors, particularly those with whom I disagree. May I pursue their best and pray for them to experience the fullness of your blessings – physically, relationally, spiritually. Change my heart that I may be faithful in this. Amen.

PONDER

1. Based on Jeremiah 29:7, what were God's intentions for the Babylonians?
2. How do you think his intentions for the Babylonians relate to those we live among today who are not yet his people?
3. In what ways does God need to change your heart so that you might more intentionally "seek the welfare of the city" where you live in exile?

For thus says the LORD of hosts, the God of Israel: Do not let your prophets and your diviners who are among you deceive you, and do not listen to the dreams that they dream, for it is a lie that they are prophesying to you in my name; I did not send them, declares the LORD. "For thus says the LORD: When seventy years are completed for Babylon, I will visit you, and I will fulfill to you my promise and bring you back to this place."

Jeremiah 29:8-10

There's too many men, too many people
Making too many problems
And there's not much love to go around
Can't you see this is the land of confusion?

Genesis, "Land of Confusion"

4

PROPHETS AND PUNDITS

N OT LONG AFTER THE JEWISH EXILES ARRIVED IN BABYLON, some of their prophets began to declare that it would only be a short time before they would return to Israel. "Just two more years and you'll be packing up your bags," said these so-called prophets. However, when Jeremiah received his word from the Lord it included a repudiation of these deceivers and their message – *"it is a lie that they are prophesying to you in my name; I did not send them, declares the Lord"* (Jeremiah 29:9). Rather than spending only more two years in exile, the Lord declared through his prophet that only when seventy years had dawned would some return to their homeland. The living among this group would most likely never see the Promised Land again. .

In every era God's people have had to tune their ears to God's voice above the noise of false prophets, political pundits, and others who have sought to influence in ways that are not in line with his Word. Today is no different. The Church in America faces several major threats from those who would use the power of their words to mislead. Some of the deceivers are deceived themselves; others are wolves in sheep's clothing. Consider the following groups that are routinely leading many Christians astray:

Religious Deceivers

These "preachers" tell their listeners that God desires for them to be materially wealthy, that they can "speak things into existence," and that they wouldn't experience illness if they had enough faith. Sometimes these messages are more veiled; other times they are spoken boldly. These "preachers" are often found on Christian TV networks and write some of the bestselling Christian books. The Apostle John warned the churches of his day, *"Beloved, do not believe every spirit, but test the spirits to see whether they are from God, for many false prophets have gone out into the world"* (1 John 4:1). We need to evaluate the words of preachers based upon how faithfully they align with God's Word.

Cultural Deceivers

These deceivers tell their listeners that either God's Word is not fully true or that when the Bible is "properly" applied to our context, certain traditional positions concerning marriage and sexuality, the atonement of Christ, or biblical authority are outdated. They view more conservative, orthodox Christians as intolerant and bigoted. When Christians are influenced by them, they fulfill what Paul wrote in 2 Timothy 4:3-4 – *"For the time is coming when people will not endure sound teaching, but having itching ears they will accumulate for themselves teachers to suit their own passions, and will turn away from listening to the truth and wander off into myths."* These kinds of false prophets are often found on social media, write influential blogs, or lead podcasts.

Political Deceivers

Christians need to be sober-minded when listening to "Christian" political pundits on both the Right and the Left. These influencers often seek to persuade their Christian listeners that their party's platform faithfully represents what Christian ethics should look like. If you listen to them long enough you may begin to espouse positions that are anti-immigrant or pro-abortion (neither of which are biblical), or you may become angry and jaded and lose your love for your neighbor who may not be a member of your political tribe. These individuals are often found on talk radio, television news programs, and the Internet.

So, how do we safeguard ourselves from these prophets and pundits? Three primary ways:

- Read and study God's Word for yourself.
- Sit under the teaching of a church with formally trained pastors.
- Ask the Holy Spirit to grant you wisdom to see the difference between truth and falsehood.

PRAYER

Father, you are the God of all truth. Jesus, you are the Truth. Holy Spirit, you desire to lead me into all truth. Open my eyes, clear my ears, tune my heart, and direct my mind to that which is of you. Grant me the wisdom to know the difference between that which sounds good and that which is good. Amen.

PONDER

1. Why do you believe the Lord was so emphatic in his repudiation of the false prophets among the Babylonian exiles?
2. Why did the Jewish exiles want to believe what the false prophets were saying? How are we often like them?
3. Which of the deceivers listed above do you find yourself most prone to being influenced by? What do you need to do to tune them out?

But our citizenship is in heaven, and from it we await a Savior, the Lord Jesus Christ.

Philippians 3:20

The only way the kingdom of God is going to be manifest in this world before Christ comes is if we manifest it by the way we live as citizens of heaven and subjects of the King.

R.C. Sproul

5

CELESTIAL STATUS

C ITIZENSHIP IS OFTEN DEFINED as holding the status of membership of a nation. Citizens are granted certain rights, privileges, and protections by the state to which they owe allegiance and duty. While citizens may have the right to vote for elected officials and make certain requests of those officials, they may also be conscripted into that nation's military and be required to observe certain laws. Being a citizen involves both push and pull between an individual and the state.

Being a citizen of a given nation is also one of the primary markers of one's identity. This may be most vividly expressed through the Olympic Games. During the opening ceremonies, members of each nation's team, blanketed by their country's colors, march into an arena as their national anthem blares through the speakers and the faithful cheer them on from all corners of the globe. Pride and patriotism are the banners flying high in the hearts of the citizens of the world's nations.

As Christians, we have a sort of dual citizenship. We are members of a particular country – the United States, Mexico, Kenya – but we also have membership in a celestial community. Paul told the church at Philippi that their *"citizenship is in heaven"* (Philippians 3:20). Though he was not calling the Philippian Christians to renounce their Roman citizenship or to rebel against Caesar, Paul wanted them to remember that their ultimate allegiance was to a heavenly commonwealth where the Lord Jesus Christ reigns. As believers living in the city of Philippi they formed a colony of another kingdom on earth. They were an outpost of heaven.

From a spiritual standpoint, followers of Christ are foreigners/exiles in the nations in which they live. The cultural norms within most countries are often opposed to or even hostile toward the values of God's people. Paul wrote that many of those who lived in Philippi walked *"as enemies of the cross of Christ. Their end is destruction, their god is their belly, and they glory in their shame, with minds that are set on earthly things"* (Philippians 3:18-19). So, when Paul declared that the Philippian Christians have a celestial citizenship, he was seeking to redirect their focus from earth to heaven. He wanted them to be more concerned with the things of Jesus than the things of Caesar. Paul desired that they live more like a "righteous" son of God and less like a "good" child of the Empire. He was hoping to persuade them to place their primary allegiance and find their principal identity in the kingdom of God, not in Rome.

God's call for us is the same today. The Lord wants us to view our identity first and foremost through the lens of being a Christian whose true citizenship is elsewhere. Only secondarily should our identity be influenced by our national citizenship, party affiliation, or ethnic background. Unfortunately, too many Christians have a misplaced understanding of their dual citizenship. Some embrace all kinds of cultural norms that are driven by earthly passions, forgetting their call to live holy lives. Others go to the opposite extreme by denying all earthly affiliations and thus rejecting their role as citizens within a nation-state. Still others seek to bring the two distinct types of citizenship together into some wretched amalgamation that approximates God and country.

There is a better way! May our lives as citizens of heaven (who happen to live on earth) look like those Olympic athletes at the opening ceremonies. May we march through the "arena" of life clothed in "colors" that clearly represent Christ – love, grace, peace, holiness, and joy – longing for the anthem of "Amazing

Grace" to be played as we join an incredible cadre of "athletes" running the race until the games are finished and the Master of Ceremonies returns. This was Paul's hope for the Church in Philippi, and it is the Lord's desire for his Church in America.

PRAYER

Father, I know I am a citizen of heaven by your grace. You alone gave me "the right to become a child of God" and, thus, a member of your kingdom (John 1:12). While I am here on earth, help me to live according to the values of our "family" and not according to the ways of the world. I pray that as an ambassador of Christ I might so well represent your kingdom that others around me might request citizenship under your reign with all the rights, privileges, and protections you bring. Amen.

PONDER

1. The kingdom of God is ruled by our Savior, the Lord Jesus Christ. How does the character of his leadership compel you to offer your full allegiance?
2. As you consider your citizenship in heaven, what rights, privileges, and protections are you most thankful for?
3. What misunderstanding of Christian dual citizenship are you most in danger of falling into? How can you best correct that?

Blessed are the peacemakers, for they
shall be called sons of God.

Matthew 5:9

Lord, make me an instrument of your peace.
Where there is hatred, let me sow love.

Francis of Assisi

6

PEACE, MAN

I N THE FIFTH CHAPTER OF HIS GOSPEL, Matthew begins his re-
cording of Jesus' Sermon on the Mount with a section com-
monly called the Beatitudes – a list of blessed actions and characteristics of God's people. Someone once described the Beatitudes
as "kingdom promises for gospel practitioners." They are assur-
ances that those who live on this earth as gospel-transformed
people will surely experience the power and blessing of relationship with Jesus both today and in the fullness of his kingdom.
However, it should be noted that the Beatitudes are not easy to
live by. They often confront our flesh at its very heart and call on
us to live quite distinctly from the world around us.

In the seventh Beatitude Jesus said, *"Blessed are the peacemakers, for they shall be called sons of God"* (Matthew 5:9). Let's unpack
this verse.

"Blessed"

This is the word that begins each of the Beatitudes. It means
"happy," "well off," or "fortunate." It is the position of those
who are in a covenant relationship with God, and in the Beatitudes it describes the condition of one favored by the Lord who
is living according to the ethics of the kingdom.

"Peacemakers"

Peacemakers are producers of peace. They get in the middle
of conflict and seek to bring it to an end. They desire to bring

wholeness of life (aka "shalom") to others through the gospel of Jesus Christ. Peacemakers help to mend the brokenness that exists between individuals and groups, but also between people and God.

"Sons of God"

This is a Semitic idiom that often indicates those who share a certain godly characteristic or status with God. The phrase "sons of God" is only used in this particular Beatitude. In some ways it is like Jesus is saying, "you most look like your Father in heaven when you take on the role of peacemaker, for he is the God of peace."

Peacemaking in Action

For Christians living in America today, the need for us to take on the role of peacemaker may be greater than at any other point in our lives. The lack of peace in our nation is almost palpable. One sees it in the eyes of those whose hearts are restless. One finds it continually via social media posts or headline news stories that demonstrate the unprecedented political polarization, growing misunderstanding and division among the races, and non-stop vitriol cast between certain interest groups. And all the while one asks, "Where are the peacemakers?" Where are the blessed sons and daughters of God to bring peace where there is none? Unfortunately, too often, Christians have found themselves engaged in these wars of words as combatants rather than as peacemakers, raising the flag of their earth-bound "tribe," forgetting their heavenly identity as they lob verbal grenades across the trenches.

Much of this misplaced focus is due to a decades-long culture war in America that Christians have effectively lost. American culture is far less influenced by Christianity today than it was in the 1980s when the most recent cultural battles began to be waged. Though the Church must continue to stand for truth and advocate for justice on the part of the vulnerable, many

Christians need to change their tactics of cultural engagement and look for opportunities to be peacemakers instead of war-mongers.

So, what might peacemaking look like? First, it involves being at peace with God. Is there unconfessed sin in my life? I should bring that before the Lord. Second, peacemaking should be focused on those I'm closest to – my family, friends, and neighbors. If there is conflict in any of those relationships, I should seek reconciliation. Third, it involves helping others to end conflict. This might be on social media or at work on in school. Helping to bring people together to graciously work through their differences and discovering the things they have in common. Last, but certainly not least, being a peacemaker means inviting others to have peace with their Creator through the gospel of Jesus Christ.

PRAYER

Father, we need your forgiveness for how we have often interacted with those with whom we disagree. Though we have desired to speak for truth, we often failed to combine it with love. Help us to see and take hold of opportunities to be peacemakers in our communities and within our society. Help us to be blessed children of God who lead others to have peace with you and peace with one another. Amen.

PONDER

1. Think back to how God has made peace with you – through the sacrificial death of Jesus, by the Spirit's initiative at your conversion, and along the way of your spiritual journey. How might that encourage you in your own pursuit of peacemaking with others?
2. Have you ever experienced the blessing of being a peacemaker? How did God use you in that circumstance?
3. Is there a relationship or a situation in which the Holy Spirit is calling you to seek peace?

Pray then like this:

"Our Father in heaven,
hallowed be your name.
Your kingdom come, your will be done,
on earth as it is in heaven.
Give us this day our daily bread,
and forgive us our debts,
as we also have forgiven our debtors.
And lead us not into temptation,
but deliver us from evil.

Matthew 6:9-13

The most important lesson we can learn is how to pray.

E.M. Bounds

7

DISPATCHES FROM THE FRONT LINES

S OMEONE ONCE SAID THAT PRAYER IS LIKE DISPATCHES from the front lines of a war. You're communicating with your "Commander," calling in for reinforcements and additional supplies, and sharing the enemy's strategies and tactics. When Paul described the spiritual weaponry associated with our battle against sin and Satan, he wrote that spiritual warriors pray *"at all times in the Spirit, with all prayer and supplication"* (Ephesians 6:18). The apostle realized that prayer is essential for gospel victory in this battle we fight in enemy territory!

Jesus knew that his disciples did not properly understand prayer. They had seen and heard prayers by the religious leaders of Israel that were often vain, bringing about no real effect. So, Jesus gave them a prayer to model. In that prayer Jesus introduced six petitions.

God's Name

Jesus begins with the receiver of our prayers – our Heavenly Father. Though prayer is a wartime dispatch, it is not sent to a detached superior, but rather to a loving Father who cares deeply for his children. The mission for which our Father has sent us involves the "hallowing" of his name. When we pray, "hallowed be your name," we are declaring that we desire that God would make his name known and that he would been properly seen in the world. The beginning of our prayer frames what follows.

God's Kingdom

The Bible describes the universal reality of all things as a conflict between the kingdom of God and the kingdoms of this world, which are influenced by Satan. From the beginning, these kingdoms of darkness have sought to undermine the work of God's kingdom. When we pray, "your kingdom come," we are asking our Father to bring about his reign and rule on this earth. His kingdom is characterized by the peace, justice, and righteousness of Christ.

God's Will

Though this petition is a continuation of "your kingdom come," it is often expressed in a more personalized way by the one who is praying. "Your will be done" is a recognition that I do not always do God's will, but I desire to do so. We are wanting to embody the ethics and values of God's kingdom through the power of Christ's Spirit dwelling within us.

Our Daily Food

Like those on the front lines, we are fully dependent on others (or for us–on Another) for the replenishment of our resources and supplies. This petition is an opportunity for us to ask from the Lord for all that we need—physically, emotionally, financially, relationally, spiritually. Our Father is the giver of every good and perfect gift (James 1:17) and he delights in providing for his children (Matthew 7:11). So, petition him daily for all you need!

Our Sins

Later in his life the Apostle Paul called himself the "chief of sinners" (1 Timothy 1:15). Though he had experienced the faithful, sanctifying work of Christ in his life, it was still clear to him that he was regularly in need of God's forgiveness for his sin. When we're humble about our need before our Father for forgiveness, it leads us to be more willing to forgive others when they have sinned against us.

Our Temptations

Ultimately, we want to honor God with our lives. We want to be faithful soldiers for Christ who never question our allegiance to the King. We ask for God's help in this when we petition for him to "lead us away from temptation." Though Christ has already delivered us from the "domain of darkness" and transferred us into his kingdom (Colossians 1:13), we still fight our battle in enemy territory with a body whose members "wage war against" against our souls (Romans 7:23). So we pray, "deliver us from evil," my Lord!

PRAYER

Today, take a few minutes to pray through the Lord's Prayer in Matthew 6:9-13, personalizing each petition.

PONDER

1. Which of the six petitions do you find yourself focusing on most in your prayers?
2. Which of the six petitions do you find yourself focusing on least in your prayers?
3. It is easy for us to lose sight of the fact that we are in the midst of a spiritual battle. How can we keep that truth at the forefront of our minds so that we see prayer as truly essential for daily victory over sin and Satan?

For the Gentiles seek after all these things, and your heavenly Father knows that you need them all. But seek first the kingdom of God and his righteousness, and all these things will be added to you.

Matthew 6:32-33

The seeking of the kingdom of God is the chief business of the Christian life.

Jonathan Edwards

8

FIRST THINGS

TAKE A MINUTE TO CONSIDER THIS QUESTION HONESTLY: when your mind is not zeroed in on a particular task, what are your thoughts most consumed by? A future spouse (hopefully, only if you're single), your kids, making money, home improvement, the world's most intractable problems, dinner/dishes/laundry, losing weight? No doubt our attention is going to be directed toward some object, idea, or goal. We are hard-wired to be pursuers, whether that be for food, for love, or for significance. Unfortunately, our pursuit of these things often causes us to experience some level of anxiety. This worry is brought on by two facts. First, we don't usually get what we want (or when we want it or how we want it). Second, if and when we do get what we want, we find that it doesn't ultimately bring satisfaction.

Jesus saw all this anxiety driven by these pursuits as completely unnecessary for the people of God. In his most extensive teaching to his disciples, he shared the following advice (Matthew 6:25-26):

> Therefore I tell you, do not be anxious about your life, what you will eat or what you will drink, nor about your body, what you will put on. Is not life more than food, and the body more than clothing? Look at the birds of the air: they neither sow nor reap nor gather into barns, and yet your heavenly Father feeds them. Are you not of more value than they?

The one who knows the Lord has no need to chase hard after the things of this life, for he has a Father in heaven who is the Provider of all things. However, since we were created to be pursuers, Jesus declared that there is something to which we can give all of our attention; something we can put all of our energies toward and that won't leave us wanting: *"But seek first the kingdom of God and his righteousness, and all these things will be added to you"* (Matthew 6:33). So, what is the "kingdom of God" and how do we seek after it?

Kingdoms are realms where sovereigns reign. They involve both the people and the area over which a king has authority. The kingdom of God is God's reign in and through his people. At present, the kingdom is manifest on earth through Spirit-filled followers of Christ who are citizens of his heavenly realm, but who live on earth in exile as ambassadors of his reign and heralds of his gospel. To seek "first" his kingdom and righteousness is to answer the question, "when your mind is not zeroed in on a particular task, what are your thoughts most consumed by?" like this: "I find my thoughts sometimes drifting toward things that aren't the most important, but what I really like to think about and what my heart is truly set on is God's glory being lived out through my life. I want other people to know Jesus and for this world to look more like he desires."

Thankfully, seeking God's kingdom is a rich and integrated occupation. We do this by carrying out our daily work in a way that honors the Lord (Colossians 3:23), by teaching our children to know and obey God's Word (Ephesians 6:4), by showing kindness to neighbors and strangers (Mark 12:31), by opening our mouths with truth that can transform (2 Corinthians 6:7), by standing as advocates for the vulnerable (Proverbs 31:8-9), by sharing what we have with others (1 Timothy 6:17-19), and by setting our gaze on Jesus (Hebrews 12:2). When we direct our energies toward these things that extend the reign of God's grace into the lives of others, Jesus says in essence, "Take a load off," don't let the things that plague other people worry you, and more specifically, "all these things (food, clothing, money, meaning, love, security) will be added to you."

So, as citizens of an unshakable, eternal kingdom let us not waste our God-given energies and Spirit-empowered giftings on temporal, earth-bound things that are less than ultimate. Let us choose to run hard after Jesus and the expansion of his love and righteousness across the globe. As Paul wrote to Timothy, "*No soldier gets entangled in civilian pursuits, since his aim is to please the one who enlisted him*" (2 Timothy 2:4).

PRAYER

Father, you are so good to me. You've freed me up to set all my attention upon you and your kingdom. I don't have to be worried about all the things everyone else is consumed by. I can be joyfully preoccupied with you. Thank you for setting me free from the anxieties of this world. Help me to keep my focus on your kingdom and your righteousness. Amen.

PONDER

1. In what ways has our Heavenly Father recently shown his provision in your life?
2. How have you seen the "Gentiles" seek after all the things of the world and be left wanting?
3. What step can you take today to be more intentional with seeking God's kingdom and righteousness first?

But Daniel resolved that he would not defile himself with the king's food, or with the wine that he drank. Therefore, he asked the chief of the eunuchs to allow him not to defile himself.

Daniel 1:8

Probably the greatest tragedy of the church throughout its long and checkered history has been its constant tendency to conform to the prevailing culture instead of developing a Christian counter-culture.

John Stott

9

COUNTERCULTURAL

THE BOOK OF DANIEL OPENS WITH THESE WORDS – *"In the third year of the reign of Jehoiakim king of Judah, Nebuchadnezzar king of Babylon came to Jerusalem and besieged it"* (Daniel 1:1). In this first encounter with Judah in 605 B.C., Nebuchadnezzar did not destroy Jerusalem; rather, he took with him some of the vessels from the Temple and some of the best of the young men and women from among the leading families – *"youths without blemish, of good appearance and skillful in all wisdom, endowed with knowledge, understanding learning, and competent to stand in the king's palace"* (Daniel 1:4). Among the young people taken were Daniel and his three buddies – Hananiah (Shadrach), Mishael (Meshach), and Azariah (Abednego). Nebuchadnezzar's goal was to "re-educate" these youths in the ways of the Babylonians with the hope that one day they would return to Judah and wisely rule as vassals of his empire.

As Daniel and his friends arrived as exiles in Babylon, they had to make a decision regarding how much they would assimilate into this foreign idolatrous culture without denying their faith in Yahweh. Quite quickly it seems Daniel determined that he would not "defile himself with the king's food." Daniel was willing to go along with the Babylonian educational program. He even took on a new name – Belteshazzar. But when it came to the food supplied by the royal table he said, "no." Why? It couldn't have been because it was sacrificed to idols (that is to read a New Testament idea into the Old). It couldn't have been because it was unclean (any food that Daniel would have eaten in Babylon would have been potentially unclean). The answer resides in the Near Eastern understanding of sharing a meal being akin to committing oneself to friendship. As James would later write, *"friendship with the world is enmity with God"* (James 4:4). This was a risky decision for Daniel. To deny the king's favor was in many respects to reject his authority. Yet, Daniel stood his ground. In the long run Daniel proved his God faithful through his courage to not become "friends" with Nebuchadnezzar.

There is no doubt that Christians in America live in a Babylon-of-sorts. Though we haven't been taken captive to another land, we live among a culture that in many respects is antithetical to Christian beliefs and values. We are consistently needing to make decisions between cultural assimilation and cultural non-conformity. Few of us believe the answer is found in living like the Amish on one hand or taking our cues from liberal "Christian" influencers on the other. The question for so many Christians is, "Where do we take our stand? What is the 'king's food' of our day?" I believe there are three critical areas in which American Christians should reject the prevailing view of the predominant culture.

Truth

In our culture today truth is individualized and relativized. The self is authoritative and determinative in the area of truth. Obviously, this idea runs completely counter to the vision of truth in the Bible, where Scripture is seen as objectively true (Psalm 119:160; 2 Peter 1:20-21) and discovered in the person of Christ (John 14:6). Jesus also declares that objective truth about God is the only thing that can set people free (John 8:32).

Sex

With objective truth out of the way, our culture has demonstrated the libertine lengths it is willing to go in the arena of sex. Christians in the West run the risk of developing a theology of sex that is not in line with Scripture. In fact, a recent survey found that half of all self-identified Christians said that casual sex was sometimes or always acceptable. Because the Bible is clear on matters of sex, Christians need to resist the cultural pressure to affirm fornication, cohabitation, homosexuality, polyamory, and transgenderism.

Human Dignity

Since sex is our culture's greatest idol, human beings are often treated as mere objects of sexual pleasure (pornography and human trafficking) or as unfortunate consequences of sexual activity that need to be discarded (abortion). Christians must continue to speak up for the voiceless and advocate for those whose rights are taken. Though the rejection of human dignity occurs in areas of our society beyond the sexual, it is most egregious here due to the pervasive nature of this cultural idolatry.

PRAYER

Father, I need the wisdom and courage of Daniel in the day in which I live, for I see "Babylon" everywhere I look. I'm not always sure what to accept and what to reject, or when to say something and when to be silent. Help me to know how to live here as a faithful ambassador of the life and ethics of your kingdom. Amen.

PONDER

1. How has your faith in God been most tested?
2. If you were Daniel, what do you think would have been the most difficult for you to accept – the change of name, the re-education program, or the king's food?
3. How does Daniel's story encourage you to live courageously in our culture?

Shadrach, Meshach, and Abednego answered and said to the king, "O Nebuchadnezzar, we have no need to answer you in this matter. If this be so, our God whom we serve is able to deliver us from the burning fiery furnace, and he will deliver us out of your hand, O king. But if not, be it known to you, O king, that we will not serve your gods or worship the golden image that you have set up."

Daniel 3:16-18

[The messengers of the gospel] must not fear men. Men can do them no harm, for the power of men ceases with the death of the body. But they overcome the fear of death with the fear of God. The danger lies not in the judgement of men, but in the judgement of God, not in the death of the body but in the eternal destruction of body and soul. Those who are still afraid of men have no fear of God, and those who have fear of God have ceased to be afraid of men. All preachers of the gospel will do well to recollect this saying daily.

Dietrich Bonhoeffer

10

INTO THE FIRE

W HAT HAPPENS WHEN AN IMMOVABLE OBJECT meets an unstoppable force? I'm not sure, but the collision is sure to make a lot of noise. That's kind of what happens in the third chapter of the Book of Daniel. Nebuchadnezzar builds an idol of gold some 90 feet tall that everyone must bow down to and worship (think "immovable object"). The only problem is that Daniel's three friends – Shadrach, Meshach, and Abednego – completely refuse to fall down before the image (think "unstoppable force"). The result is as you would expect: King Nebuchadnezzar gets really ticked off and decides to throw them into a furnace heated seven times its normal temperature. The three Jewish young men's response is classic – "Our God will deliver us. But even if he doesn't, we're still not worshipping your gods." In the end, they are delivered by a "fourth man" in the fire who has an appearance "like a son of the gods."

The story of God's persecuted people hasn't always ended with physical deliverance. As Hebrews 13:35-37 reads, "*Some were tortured, refusing to accept release, so that they might rise again to a better life. Others suffered mocking and flogging, and even chains and imprisonment. They were stoned, they were sawn in two, they were killed with the sword.*" The history of the Church has told a similar story. Yet, for each Christian who has experienced persecution, God's promise to never leave or forsake them has been realized.

The question for us today is, "Are we willing to suffer for the sake of Christ and the gospel? Are we willing to endure persecution because of the name of Jesus?" Though this question hasn't had to be answered by many Christians in the United States, that may not always be the case. As Christian martyr Dietrich Bonhoeffer would attest, nations can quickly turn against followers of Christ. So, how do we better prepare our hearts and minds for persecution that might come? I think there are three ways.

Embrace The Fact That Persecution Is To Be An Expected Part Of The Christian Experience.

In his second letter to his protégé Timothy, the Apostle Paul wrote: *"Therefore do not be ashamed of the testimony about our Lord, nor of me his prisoner, but share in suffering for the gospel by the power of God,"* and *"all who desire to live a godly life in Christ Jesus will be persecuted"* (2 Timothy 1:8, 3:12). To the Philippian church, Paul wrote, *"For it has been granted to you that for the sake of Christ you should not only believe in him but also suffer for his sake"* (Philippians 1:29). Suffering for the gospel was common in the first century and continues to be common in many places around the world today.

Choose To Make Regular Sacrifices That Require You To Lose Something.

Jesus told his disciples to take up their cross *daily* and follow him (Luke 9:23). Each day there is something for the sake of Christ that we can offer that costs us -- our time, our money, our attention, our reputation, our comfort. The more we do this on a regular basis, the more God can trust us to be faithful when much more is demanded of us because of our faith.

Read Accounts of Modern-Day Persecution And Pray For Those Being Mistreated.

Other people's stories encourage us – especially when those stories prove God to be faithful through our trials and difficulties. When we hear of their strength, we believe that God can enable us to persevere as well. The Lord calls us to not only be strengthened by others' stories but to strengthen persecuted brothers and sisters through our prayers (Romans 15:3-31; 2 Thessalonians 3:1-3). Two places where you can read stories of the persecuted and pray for them can be found at the following websites: opendoorsusa.org and persecution.com.

PRAYER

Jesus, I want to be willing to stand for you – in my school, in my work-place, in my community, among my friends and family. At times I wonder what other people might think if I bring up your name or share the story of your life with others. Help me to have courage to bear the name of Christ regardless of what people might say. Help me also to not bow down to the idols of our culture, even if it costs me something. Amen.

PONDER

1. What do Shadrach, Meshach, and Abednego's words in Daniel 3:16-18 say about their belief in Yahweh?
2. What do you believe led these three young men to express such courage?
3. Can you think of a time in your life when it was difficult to bear the name of Christ? How did you respond?

These all died in faith, not having received the things promised, but having seen them and greeted them from afar, and having acknowledged that they were strangers and exiles on the earth. If they had been thinking of that land from which they had gone out, they would have had opportunity to return. But as it is, they desire a better country, that is, a heavenly one. Therefore God is not ashamed to be called their God, for he has prepared for them a city.

Hebrews 11:13-16

Certainly there was an Eden on this very unhappy earth. We all long for it, and we are constantly glimpsing it: our whole nature at its best and least corrupted, its gentlest and most humane, is still soaked with the sense of 'exile.'

J.R.R. Tolkien

11

A HOME AWAY FROM HOME

T HE ELEVENTH CHAPTER OF HEBREWS has often been referred to
as the "hall of faith," for it provides an account of the faithfulness of some of the Old Testament's most recognized saints –
Abraham, Sarah, Isaac, Jacob, Joseph, Moses, and others. These
men and women had come to the resolute conclusion that their
God was not only alive, but a rewarder of those who seek him
(Hebrew 11:6). In addition, the more they turned to the Lord and
identified with him, the more they realized that the earth was not
their true home. They were pilgrims in this life awaiting the
promises of the next. Even once they had entered Canaan – the
"land of promise" – it was still evident to them that their true
home was elsewhere. So long as they were on this earth they
would be "strangers and exiles" because their true home was a
heavenly one (Hebrews 11:4). As commentator F.F. Bruce writes,
"The earthly Canaan and the earthly Jerusalem were but temporary object lessons pointing to the saints' everlasting rest, the
well-founded city of God."

You and I as followers of Christ await that same home as the
Hebrew saints who went before us. We, too, are sojourners and
exiles on this earth (1 Peter 2:11). However, I realize it doesn't
always feel like that. Sometimes this place can feel pretty comfortable. Maybe there's a place in the mountains that resets your
spirit and refreshes your soul. Maybe you have a memory from
childhood that brings you back to a time you felt loved and protected. Maybe there is some person in whose presence you feel

completely secure. Those momentary feelings of peace and joy and comfort that we receive from some place or person this side of heaven are blessed signposts of the enduring home we will have with Jesus. And that is what we should long for – a realm of shalom that is under the gracious reign of our King, full of righteousness and love; a new Eden in which there is no sin or no suffering, with reconciliation between all nations and their God. Christ has redeemed us for such a place and we should long for it. In thinking about this kingdom to come, the Scottish poet Henry Francis Lyte penned these words:

> *It is not for me to be seeking my bliss*
> *And building my hope in a region like this;*
> *I look for a city which hands have not piled,*
> *I pant for a country by sin undefiled.*

So, while we are here awaiting that blessed country, how might we live faithfully as strangers and exiles? A few thoughts:

- Let your first identity be your Christian identity – not your ethnic, national, political, or denominational identity.
- Don't get overly frustrated by the ways this land proves it isn't our home (injustice, conflict, irrationality, chaos).
- *"Seek first the kingdom of God and his righteousness"* (Matthew 6:33). Don't first seek wealth, position, power, pleasure, personal comfort, the perfect home, or the most "likes."
- Spend more time with Jesus (prayer, Word, his people) – he is the One who truly constitutes our future "home" in the new heavens and new earth (Revelation 21:1).
- Be on guard with becoming too "Corinthian." The things we watch and listen to, and the people we spend time with, really do affect our hearts and souls.
- Lastly, sing songs about the glory to come. There's hardly anything that causes our anticipation of our true home to grow like the words of heavenward worship songs.

PRAYER

Heavenly Father, I realize that this place is not my home. However, sometimes I get overly comfortable here. I lose sight of the fact that you have prepared for me a city that is far greater than anything I could experience here. I pray you would help me to desire that "better country" where I will dwell with you. May I remember that my citizenship is elsewhere and live as a holy ambassador while I am here. In Jesus' name, Amen.

PONDER

1. For what reason was *"God not ashamed to be called* [Abraham, Sarah, Isaac, and Jacob's] *God"* (Hebrews 11:16)?
2. Many of the saints mentioned in Hebrews 11 actually lived as foreigners in lands not their own. How does living in a place where one is not native help cultivate one's identity as a spiritual exile?
3. Which characteristics or practices most evidence a Christian who lives like an exile on this earth?

To those who are elect exiles of the Dispersion in Pontus, Galatia, Cappadocia, Asia, and Bithynia, according to the foreknowledge of God the Father, in the sanctification of the Spirit, for obedience to Jesus Christ and for sprinkling with his blood: May grace and peace be multiplied to you.

1 Peter 1:1-2

He ran till he came to a small hill, at the top of which stood a cross and at the bottom of which was a tomb. I saw in my dream that when Christian walked up the hill to the cross, his burden came loose from his shoulders and fell off his back, tumbling down the hill until it came to the mouth of the tomb, where it fell in to be seen no more.

John Bunyan, of Christian in The Pilgrim's Progress

12
A PILGRIM'S POSITION

THE POLLS SEEM TO BE CONCLUSIVE – anxiety is on the rise. A world of ever-increasing uncertainty has led to growing levels of disquiet. If we're honest with ourselves, we've felt it too; no one is immune. We have all faced these feelings of nervousness, or even sometimes panic, as we look at the world around us. Some of that concern is directly tied to the fact that we live in an age and location in which the Christian faith is increasingly seen as strange or extreme. We wonder what freedoms we might lose in the days ahead or what trials our children could face because they follow Jesus.

When Peter opened his letter to the churches of Asia Minor (modern-day Turkey), he was writing to a group of Christians who were clearly viewed as outsiders. He even calls them "exiles" or "sojourners" or "pilgrims." Though they may have been born in the cities in which they found themselves and even had the rights of citizens, it was evident to all that they didn't belong. And the foreignness of their faith was leading many to experience discrimination and other forms of persecution from their neighbors. In light of their suffering, Peter sought to encourage them by reminding them of several truths regarding their position in Christ as "elect" exiles.

First, he says our election for salvation was *"according to the foreknowledge of the Father."* These believers in Asia Minor and all others had been chosen by God for a relationship with him through Jesus Christ. This choosing was not the Christian's doing; this was God's work alone, done by his grace. The Father had set his covenantal affection upon them. Though election should not elicit pride in believers' hearts, it should bring a level of comfort that God is for them and with them. Trusting in the Father's presence and relational favor is especially needed in seasons of difficulty when our experience can lead us to question the Lord's thoughts toward us.

Second, Peter states that their election was accomplished through *"the sanctification of the Spirit."* The Spirit of God had been promised by the prophets before Christ (Ezekiel 37:14, Joel 2:28) and now those who trusted Christ were being filled with the Spirit and made holy by him. That's what Peter meant by "sanctification" – the Holy Spirit graciously invaded our lives and converted us from sinful rebels into righteous children. And the Spirit continues his work of transformation throughout our lives, empowering us to live as God's distinct, set-apart people.

Third, Peter writes that God's choosing was for the purpose of *"obedience to Jesus Christ and for sprinkling with his blood."* Obedience in this passage entails the "obedience of faith" at our conversion (Romans 1:5), but it also involves our ongoing surrender to Christ. For these Christians in Asia Minor and for many throughout the generations, their obedience would require suffering, just as it had for Christ himself. Interestingly, Paul in his letter to the church at Philippi would link God's election for salvation with his gracious determination of suffering in the lives of believers (Philippians 1:29). What Peter and Paul were both seeking to do was provide their readers with confidence in God's sovereign goodness in the midst of their crucibles.

Though none of us knows the future we will face as Christians in the West, we can take heart that through the cross of Jesus Christ we have been declared to be victors over all things because nothing on this earth (or in the heavens) could ever remove us from God's loving presence (Romans 8:31-39). As 1 Peter 1:1-2 powerfully displays, the full measure of the Trinity (Father, Son, and Holy Spirit) is at work in our lives. We have nothing to fear. May grace and peace be multiplied to you in abundance, my friend.

PRAYER

Father, what amazing truths for me to behold! You are so good to me. I know I don't deserve your love, but I receive it. I find courage and comfort in the life-giving work of your Spirit. Christ's blood applied to my life grants me the confidence I need to approach you openly and at all times. Your favor toward me is the greatest gift I could ever receive. May all these truths lead me to be fearless in the face of evil, for you prepare a table before me in the presence of my enemies. Amen.

PONDER

1. Some have viewed God's "election" through a negative lens. How do you see it after studying this passage?
2. Which truth from Peter's opening words provides the most comfort to you?
3. Can you think of anyone who is presently paralyzed by fear or anxiety? Pray for them through this passage and consider sharing it with them.

But you are a chosen race, a royal priesthood, a holy nation, a people for his own possession, that you may proclaim the excellencies of him who called you out of darkness into his marvelous light.

1 Peter 2:9

To be elect in Christ Jesus means to be incorporated into his mission to the world, to be the bearer of God's saving purpose for his whole world.

Lesslie Newbigen

13

IDENTITY POLITICS

O VER THE PAST FEW YEARS, the term *identity politics* has become commonplace. Identity politics is the practice of some groups who have a particular racial, religious, ethnic, social, or cultural identity to promote their own specific interests or concerns with less attention given to the interests or concerns of any larger political group. The LGBTQ+ community and other groups on the political Left have often been described as employing identity politics. At times, groups on the Right, like Evangelical Christians, have also been described this way.

In 1 Peter 2:9, the Apostle Peter was calling the churches of Asia Minor to participate in identity politics of a different order. Their "identity" and "politics" were to be centered on their membership in the kingdom of God for the glory of Christ among the nations. Whereas the identity politics practiced within America's political landscape today are self-centered, the identity politics of the kingdom are centered on God and others.

In this verse, Peter describes Christians with four identity markers that not only set them apart *from* the world but also describe their calling *in* the world – a chosen race, a royal priesthood, a holy nation, a people for his own possession. The Church in many respects was taking on the calling that Israel had been given at Sinai (Exodus 19:5-6). Peter writes that God has given Christ's followers this status for the purpose of *"proclaiming the excellencies of him who called you out of darkness into his marvelous light."* Their distinct identity was to lead to worship and mission.

Chosen Race

The Church is comprised of God's elect people – both Jew and Gentile. Our chosenness is dependent on being identified with Christ. Paul writes in Ephesians 2:13-15, *"But now in Christ Jesus you who were once far off have been brought near by the blood of Christ. For he himself is our peace, who has made us both one and has broken down in his flesh the dividing wall of hostility … that he might create in himself one new man in place of two."* What an amazing privilege we have as God's "chosen race" – that is, his people. We now have a spiritual "ethnicity" that supersedes our natural ethnicity.

Royal Priesthood

If you've ever had the privilege of visiting England, you quickly come to realize the royal family is a pretty big deal - they own castles throughout the realm, their faces are printed on British notes, and the leader of the family is even called "The Sovereign." The House of Windsor is unlike any other family in all of the United Kingdom, but they're not unlike other royals. Royalty has always been exclusive, unapproachable, unattainable. For that reason, it is quite interesting for Peter to describe the Church of Jesus Christ as a *royal* "priesthood" because priests are meant to be inclusive, approachable, and receptive. Priests not only represent God to people by their holiness, but they also represent people to God through service and sacrifice. Priests are intercessors and mediators. This is the amazing truth – our membership in the household of the King, our royalty, should lead to the service of others.

Holy Nation

Like Israel before it, the Church is to be a people set apart for God's purposes. Christians from every country around the world now comprise a new "nation" that is not bound by borders. Being a holy nation involves not only a level of Spirit-empowered practical righteousness, but also a missional identity of being sent into the world with the Word and work of the gospel. The Lord has redeemed us as a people for himself to bear the image of Christ throughout the world that we may *"make disciples of all nations"* (Matthew 28:19).

People For His Own Possession

We belong to Jesus! As 1 Corinthians 6:19-20 says, *"You are not your own, for you were bought with a price."* Christ paid the ultimate price for us through the shedding of his blood on the cross. This was the most disproportionate transaction in history. No one had ever overpaid so much. Our response to his sacrifice is thankfulness that leads to worship, and worship that leads to witness – that we may *"proclaim the excellences of him who called us out of darkness into his marvelous light."*

PRAYER

Father, we are not deserving of any of these titles that you have bestowed on your Church. It is only by grace and the work of your Son that we could be called your people. We want to not only embrace the unbelievable favor you have given us, but also live in light of our identity in Christ. You have truly called us "out of darkness and into your marvelous light." May we walk in your light and shine like the Light of the World. Amen.

PONDER

1. How was each member of the Trinity involved in calling you "out of darkness?"
2. Which of the titles from 1 Peter 2:9 mean the most to you as an exile? Why?
3. In what ways is God calling you to "proclaim his excellencies" today?

Beloved, I urge you as sojourners and exiles
to abstain from the passions of the flesh, which
wage war against your soul. Keep your conduct
among the Gentiles honorable, so that when
they speak against you as evildoers, they
may see your good deeds and glorify God
on the day of visitation.

1 Peter 2:11-12

The knowledge that [Christians] do not belong
does not lead to withdrawal, but to taking
their standards of behavior, not from the culture
in which they live, but from their "home" culture
of heaven, so that their life always fits
the place they are headed to, rather than
their temporary lodging in this world.

Peter H. Davids

14

YOUR HONOR

C HRISTIANS HAVE ALWAYS BEEN A PECULIAR PEOPLE, often viewed as strange by the non-Christians they live among. This was definitely the case of the early Church among the Roman populace. Writing in the early second century, the Roman historian Suetonius described Christians as "a class of people animated by a novel and dangerous superstition." Christian ethics (particularly in the realm of sexuality and marriage) were often seen as overly severe. Christian practices (prayer, the Lord's Supper, giving to the poor) were routinely labeled as the ways of the ignorant or the rituals of the superstitious.

The Church was also viewed as narrow-minded because of their lack of participation in the worship of local deities. One may remember the riot that was caused in Ephesus when craftsmen of the shrine to Artemis observed that their business was shrinking because fewer people were buying their wares (Acts 19:21-41). One of the leading silversmiths, Demetrius, declared, *"this Paul has persuaded and turned away a great many people, saying that gods made with hands are not gods. And there is danger not only that this trade of ours may come into disrepute but also that the temple of the great goddess Artemis may be counted as nothing"* (Acts 19:26-27). The Christian faith was disrupting the economics and social conventions of Ephesus and this was leading some to slander the followers of Christ as evildoers.

In his first letter to the churches throughout Asia Minor, the Apostle Peter provides an answer for the hostility many Christians in the region were facing. He urged them not to assimilate and give in to customs of their communities, but rather to *"abstain from the passions of the flesh"* (which were oftentimes in concert with the ethics of Roman culture) and to live honorably among the Gentiles. Christians were to remember that they were sojourners and exiles among the predominant culture. Their home in heaven and their identity as God's people ought to lead them to live distinctly for missional purposes, that the unbelievers among them would *"see [their] good deeds and glorify God on the day of visitation"* (1 Peter 2:12). The hope was that somehow the quality of their holy living would be a means of bringing worship to Christ by the Gentiles – either through the conversion of unbelievers in this life or by the recognition of their error at the day of judgment.

Today, Christians in the West need to heed Peter's exhortations to live differently than the culture. Too often we have accepted conclusions that Christians are narrow-minded and intolerant, leading us to acquiesce to the predominant culture's views on cohabitation, sexuality, transgenderism, and abortion. These issues around the expression of one's sexuality are like the Artemis worship of Ephesus. They are our culture's primary "local" deities. And when they are threatened, crowds will assemble to either demand our allegiance or call for our "cancellation."

If Peter were carrying on a lengthier discussion with us about *"keeping our conduct among the Westerners honorable,"* he would probably note the significance of not only abstaining from the practice and acceptance of sexual sin, but also the need to express tender mercy to all of those involved. Our "good deeds" the world around us sees are not primarily the restriction of certain cultural norms, but rather the gracious ways in which we extend Christ's love to a world that is under God's judgment, as we once were ourselves.

PRAYER

Father in Heaven, you have called us out of darkness and into your marvelous light. You desire for us to live in a way that leads us to greater fellowship with you, not in ways that wage war against our souls. We pray that you would help us to live as foreigners in this place – as a people with distinct customs and ethics. Though this may make us seem strange to those who live near us, we pray that our uniqueness would lead our neighbors to see your exceptional character and bring praise to your Name. Amen.

PONDER

1. In what ways does it bring you comfort that Jesus was also maligned and spoken of as an evildoer?
2. Which *"passion of the flesh"* that our culture propagates do you find yourself most susceptible to accepting?
3. Pray for an unbeliever who has opportunity to observe your good deeds to no longer slander the name of Christ but begin to praise God because of the grace he offers all.

Be subject for the Lord's sake to every human institution, whether it be to the emperor as supreme, or to governors as sent by him to punish those who do evil and to praise those who do good. For this is the will of God, that by doing good you should put to silence the ignorance of foolish people.

1 Peter 2:13-15

When the church aligns itself politically, it gives priority to the compromises and temporal successes of the political world rather than its Christian confession of eternal truth. And when the church gives up its rightful place as the conscience of the culture, the consequences for society can be horrific.

Chuck Colson

15

SWAMP PEOPLE

THERE IS A GROWING ANTI-GOVERNMENT STREAK alive and well in the American Church today. It stems from a lack of trust in institutions in general, but it is especially directed toward the political realm. Much of the distaste is driven by a sense that our representatives are out of touch with the actual needs and interests of most Americans. This mistrust is further compounded by the growing polarization and tribalism between Progressives and Conservatives. Though some of our frustration with our elected officials and government in general may be warranted, our response to this dissatisfaction has often led us toward attitudes and behaviors that are not in line with a biblical ethic. We have too often become cynical and divisive.

Peter's first example regarding how to live faithfully as aliens and sojourners is concerned with our relationship to the state. He told the churches in Asia Minor to *"be subject for the Lord's sake to every institution"* including those in positions of governmental authority – the emperor and governors (1 Peter 2:13-14). In Peter's day there was no such thing as a Christian congressman or a Protestant president. All the leaders in power throughout the Empire worshipped the Roman gods and many, if not most, were oppressive toward groups and individuals that were not in line with Roman way, including the followers of Jesus. Those who lived throughout the Empire were not protected by anything like a Bill of Rights. One's rights were mostly determined by the whims of those in power. And yet, Christians were to "be subject" to their state leaders.

The apostle's call for Christians to submit to political leaders was guided by two truths: 1) doing so will honor the Lord, and 2) doing so will silence their opponents. First, when Christians place themselves under the authority of the government, they ultimately place themselves under the authority of Christ. The reason for this was that every authority has been instituted by God (Romans 13:1-2). However, since their submission is first to the Lord, Christians would not be encouraged, let alone required, to obey commands that clearly transgress God's expressed will. Second, it is God's will for his people to be subject to the governing authorities *"that by doing good you should put to silence the ignorance of foolish people"* (1 Peter 2:13-15). By not being labeled as anti-government by the broader populace, Christians help to quiet the slander that they are not good citizens. That slander was leading to deeper expressions of persecution on the churches in Asia Minor.

Thankfully, we do not live in Asia Minor in the first century. We live in a land that has as many protections for its citizens as any in history. The first section of the 1st Amendment to our Constitution states, "Congress shall make no law respecting an establishment of religion, or prohibiting the free exercise thereof." The framers of our Constitution had lived under a regime that demanded allegiance to its brand of Christianity and they wanted to ensure that Americans were free to worship as they saw fit. Though we must be vigilant to see that this right is continually secured, we ought also to recognize the blessed position we find ourselves in as Christians in America.

To be faithful to Peter's command found in these verses, I believe Christians should take the following six steps:

- Be thankful for the freedoms we do have.
- Pray for our governmental leaders.
- Ask the Lord to bring change to our society where needed.
- Vote and be involved in government where we can.

- Avoid being influenced by groups that are anti-government (either Left or Right).
- Cultivate hope by setting our eyes more on Christ's kingdom than on the kingdoms of this world.

PRAYER

Father, it's often difficult for us to trust people, especially people in power. However, we know we can trust you and your Word that tells us to yield to our governing authorities. May we honor you as we submit to governors and representatives and presidents – some who know you and many others who do not. Let our lives of service and submission be a sign that you are our King. Amen.

PONDER

1. What do you learn about God from this passage?
2. "Foolish people" in verse 15 seem to be on all sides of this issue. How so?
3. Is your present posture toward our government in line with Peter's admonition?

But in your hearts honor Christ the Lord
as holy, always being prepared to make
a defense to anyone who asks you for
a reason for the hope that is in you;
yet do it with gentleness and respect.

1 Peter 3:15

To be a soul winner is the happiest thing
in this world.

Charles Spurgeon

16

WITNESS PROTECTION

I F YOU'VE EVER VISITED A LOCATION in a foreign country where Americans rarely travel, you probably noticed that the locals were intrigued by your presence. They may have been interested in what brought you to their area or asked questions about life in the US. Being from Texas, one question I have been asked was whether most people still traveled by horse (I guess they had seen a few Westerns). As citizens of another "land," our peculiar ways as Christian exiles may lead others to question what makes us different and the reasons behind those differences.

Peter told the churches of Asia Minor to be ready for such inquiries—"*always be prepared to make a defense to anyone who asks you for a reason for the hope that is in you*" (1 Peter 3:15). However, when many Christians read these words, they are terrified by them. "ALWAYS be prepared to make a DEFENSE to ANYONE who asks you for a REASON for the HOPE that is within you" – yikes! But this command shouldn't scare us. What Peter was writing to the Christians in Asia Minor in his day and what the Spirit is continuing to speak to us in our day is something every disciple can do, so long as they are willing. Let me share how.

A Good Defense

First, know that we perform this kind of defending and reasoning all the time, just with things that are typically not connected to our faith. When we explain why we prefer Target to Walmart, we engage in this kind of activity. When we argue for the supremacy of our favorite sports team, we show our ability to give a reasoned defense. Just about anyone could participate in a discussion about the beach vs. the mountains or Macs vs. PCs. In these examples we typically share some measure of *objective* information and some measure of *subjective* information. *Objective* relates to facts; *subjective* relates to experience or opinion. As we "make a defense" we should feel confident to share both.

God's Story

Second, you are probably already familiar with the *objective* basics of the gospel story. God created everything including us > Man sinned and the world was changed for the worse > God loved people so much that he sent Jesus to save us from sin > Jesus lived, died on a cross, and rose from the grave to offer people true life > Those who put their trust in Christ receive forgiveness and life. Most Christians know these basic truths. However, their concern arises with the thought that these truths might be further questioned. Though I think it is helpful for Christians to be able to provide additional evidence for these facts, it is not essential. Very few people are honestly questioning the validity of the objective nature of the biblical story. Most who strongly doubt these facts have already made up their minds and wouldn't be swayed by even the most convincing of arguments.

Your Story

Third, your own personal story of how God changed your life will include both *objective* and *subjective* elements. This is called your testimony. All testimonies have a BEFORE, a HOW and an AFTER. First, your BEFORE is what your life was like prior to meeting Christ. It doesn't need to be involve a laundry list of sins to be strong. My BEFORE is simply that I was a kid who didn't come from a Christian home. Next, your testimony involves a HOW – the circumstances involved when you were led to faith. Some HOWs involve the gospel being preached at church or a friend sharing the Good News with you. Regardless of the means, this is when you heard about the death and resurrection of Jesus and you placed your trust in him. Lastly, the AFTER is how your life is different since you were saved. When I speak of my AFTER, I usually mention the presence of God's faithfulness, provision, and peace in my life. Testimonies have a lot of power these days because people place a lot of weight on subjective experience.

Gentleness And Respect

Fourth, Peter writes that our answer to questions regarding our faith should be done with "gentleness and respect." How appropriate are these words today! Because "gentleness and respect" are lacking in much of our public discourse, their presence will be noticed and appreciated. Sharing our faith with "gentleness and respect" also demonstrates that, ultimately, we believe that it is God's work to convince someone of the veracity of what we believe. We don't need to be overly persuasive or exceptionally intelligent; we simply need faithfulness and a measure of courage.

PRAYER

Jesus, we want to set you apart as Lord of our lives. One area in which we need greater surrender to you is with our witness of the gospel. Too often we have been unwilling to share you with others, scared of what people might think or worried that we would not have the right words. Forgive us, Lord, and lead us to deeper levels of faithfulness and intention because of the hope you have given us. Amen.

PONDER

1. How is honoring Christ as holy connected to the sharing of our faith?
2. What part of evangelism most scares you? How might you gain victory over that fear?
3. Spend a few minutes asking the Lord to grant you the opportunity to witness to some specific people.

Finally, be strong in the Lord and in the strength of his might. Put on the whole armor of God, that you may be able to stand against the schemes of the devil. For we do not wrestle against flesh and blood, but against the rulers, against the authorities, against the cosmic powers over this present darkness, against the spiritual forces of evil in the heavenly places. Therefore, take up the whole armor of God, that you may be able to withstand in the evil day, and having done all, to stand firm.

Ephesians 6:10-13

"Christ in you, the hope of glory." I'm not afraid of the devil. The devil can handle me – he's got judo I never heard of. But he can't handle the One to whom I'm joined; he can't handle the One to whom I'm united; he can't handle the One whose nature dwells in my nature.

A.W. Tozer

17

TURF WAR

A S CHRISTIANS, WE HAVE TURNED AWAY from the kingdom of this world and have given our allegiance to King Jesus. Though we no longer yield to the kingdom of darkness, we still live within its realm. And because of that, Satan as *"god of this world"* (2 Corinthians 4:4) seeks to bring war against us rebels. As Paul writes, *"we do not wrestle against flesh and blood, but against the rulers, against the authorities, against the cosmic powers over this present darkness, against the spiritual forces of evil in the heavenly places"* (Ephesians 6:12). Our battle is a spiritual one that simultaneously takes place on earth and in the heavens. It involves supernatural "rulers," "authorities," "powers," and "forces." If only we had eyes to see, right? On second thought...

Since we trust in the veracity of God's Word, we accept these words from Ephesians 6 as true. However, if we're honest, most of the time we live oblivious to any cosmic spiritual battle in our daily lives. We wake up, get ourselves ready for the day, go about our day, get ready for bed, go to sleep, and repeat. Demonic rulers and authorities seem to be the least of our concern. Our lives appear to be far more affected by our spouse and children, our supervisor and employees, our neighbors and civic leaders. Yet, Paul declares that our primary struggle in this life is not one against flesh and blood (Ephesians 6:12). We need to let that sink in: human beings, because they are flesh and blood creatures, are not our proper enemies. In this era of outrage in which hatred is so commonplace, Christians must reset their minds to love their fellow man and shift their righteous anger toward their true Adversary.

In addition, we also need to better recognize the tactics the Enemy uses to wage war against us. Paul calls these "the schemes of the devil" (Ephesians 6:11) because of his use of subterfuge. Some of Satan's primary strategies involve *deception* (leading believers to accept falsehood), *temptation* (leading believers to give in to sin), and *accusation* (leading believers to question their standing before God). Thankfully, Paul describes how Christ's followers can powerfully respond to these attacks. Let's look at the three commands:

Be Strong In The Lord

Our power to wage spiritual warfare against the demonic forces is found "in the strength of [Jesus'] might," not in our own abilities (Ephesians 6:10). We gain access to Christ's strength through the indwelling presence of the Holy Spirit. The more we abide in Christ and his Word, the greater our capacity to access the Lord's spiritual reserves. This is one of the reasons why regular Bible reading, Scripture memory, and prayer should be a part of every Christian's normal rhythms.

Take Up The Whole Armor Of God

In Ephesians 6:14-18, Paul goes on to vividly describe the various elements of spiritual defense and offense that we are to employ in this fight – the belt of truth, the breastplate of righteousness, shoes fitted with the gospel of peace, the shield of faith, the helmet of salvation, the sword of the Spirit, and prayer. Christians ought to ensure that they are taking each piece of this armor into their daily lives, for if any piece is missing, that is surely where the Enemy will attack.

Stand Firm

One of the most consistent commands from God to his people has been, "be strong and courageous." Because God is with us (even *in* us), we have no need to fear the war or those spiritual forces who attack us. In fact, we can have confidence that "no weapon formed against us shall prosper" (Isaiah 54:17) and that we are "more than conquerors through him who loved us" (Romans 8:37). So, stand firm, my friend!

PRAYER

Lord Jesus, you fight my battles. You have already gained victory through your death and resurrection. And, because your Spirit dwells within me I can wage war alongside you. May I have spiritual eyes to see when the Enemy is attacking me and others so that I may utilize all the weaponry you have given me to fight with all your power. Be glorified in me, Jesus. Amen.

PONDER

1. We are told to be strong "in the Lord's might." What aspect of the Lord's strength do you most need in your battle today?
2. Which of Satan's strategies is he employing most in your life right now – deception, temptation, or accusation?
3. In what way do you need to shift your focus from flesh and blood enemies to true spiritual enemies? How can you pray for or bless the flesh and blood people you have considered to be enemies?

Remember that you were at that time separated from Christ, alienated from the commonwealth of Israel and strangers to the covenants of promise, having no hope and without God in the world. But now in Christ Jesus you who once were far off have been brought near by the blood of Christ. For he himself is our peace, who has made us both one and has broken down in his flesh the dividing wall of hostility by abolishing the law of commandments expressed in ordinances, that he might create in himself one new man in place of the two, so making peace.

Ephesians 2:12-15

The reason we haven't solved the race problem in America after hundreds of years is that people apart from God are trying to create unity, while people under God who already have unity are not living out the unity we possess. The result of both of these conditions is disastrous for America. Our failure to find cultural unity as a nation is directly related to the church's failure to preserve our spiritual unity. The church has already been given unity because we've been made part of the same family.

John Perkins

18

ONE BLOOD

ONE OF THE GREATEST CHALLENGES THE AMERICAN CHURCH faces today is that of racial reconciliation and racial unity among those in Christ. America's past, filled with chattel slavery and Jim Crow-era policies, still lingers today. America's present, influenced by critical race theory on one side and an unwilling-ness to acknowledge racial injustice on the other side, makes healing all the more difficult. Christians in America need to look at race and racial conflicts through the lens of the gospel. If we will approach this subject with a healthy blend of compassion and truth, seeking to build bridges with one another, I believe the Church can provide a picture of the unifying power of Christ. If we ignore these issues or fail to pursue them with grace, I fear these problems will grow ever more.

It is important to remember that this isn't the first time Chris-tians have needed to confront ethnic divisions in the Church and in the broader culture. We oftentimes forget the early days of the faith were fraught with conflict between Jews and Gentiles. His-torically, the Jews thought of the Gentiles as being a little less than dogs and many of the Gentiles saw the Jews as religious fanatics. In the days of Jesus and the early church, it didn't help that the Romans had control over Israel and frequently mistreat-ed the Jews. So, when Romans and other Gentiles started to re-ceive the gospel and enter the community of the faithful, many Jews objected. In fact, the first Church council, which took place in Jerusalem, was held over the question of whether Gentiles could be freely admitted to the Church or whether they must take on Jewish identity first (Acts 15).

In Ephesians 2, Paul, writing some 12 years after the Jerusalem Council, addresses how the past division between Jews and Gentiles has now become unity in Christ. As we seek to be peacemakers and racial reconcilers within the Church and within the broader culture, we would do well to consider these two truths.

The Blood Of Christ Is The Great Unifier of Christians.

"But now in Christ Jesus you who once were far off have been brought near by the blood of Christ" (Ephesians 2:13). Every race has common ancestors in Adam and Eve. Because of our common ancestor, we also have a common moral dilemma – sin. *"None is righteous, no, not one,"* says Romans 3:10. There is no righteous race, people, ethnicity, or culture. Sin has bound all of us as slaves and led us all to rebel against our Creator. Thus, we needed a common Savior. Paul writes that Jesus' blood – which represents both his person and his work – is the one thing that can unify people in a way that is righteous. Christian, Christ alone is the hope of true racial reconciliation.

Our Common Identity In Christ Is Greater Than Our Racial Differences.

"For he himself is our peace, who has made us both one and has broken down in his flesh the dividing wall of hostility" (Ephesians 2:14). Because I have been redeemed by the gospel of Jesus Christ, I must now view my identity primarily through my common family in Christ. If I choose to continue to put my race or nationality first, I deny that Christ has made the races one through his blood. I am first a Christian, before I am a White American with British and Choctaw heritage. This doesn't mean that I cannot express myself through my racial and cultural identity. No, Jesus loves the beautiful variety of peoples he has redeemed. However, if my racial identity or culture causes me to minimize the unity I have with my brothers and sisters in Christ

who are from diverse ethnic backgrounds, then I need to reject those aspects of my background.

Peace Is Possible.

"...that he might create in himself one new man in place of the two, so making peace" (Ephesians 2:15). So many of you are deeply discouraged by the racial divides you see in the Church and within our nation. I am too. However, I cannot allow my discouragement to lead me to apathy or inaction. Peace between all races and all peoples is possible – especially for those who have been transformed by Jesus. Let us pray for the Lord to bring peace and let us be willing to be his peacemakers.

PRAYER

Jesus, through your cross you have broken down the "dividing wall of hostility" that existed between Jew and Gentile. You have made peace possible not only between them, but between every race and people. Through the gospel Indians can love Pakistanis, Irish can hold hands with English, Serbs can welcome Kosovars, and without a doubt Black Americans and White Americans can live in harmony. Amen.

PONDER

1. In your own words, how would you describe what Jesus accomplished between the races through his death?
2. Which of the three truths listed above do you most need to remember?
3. How can you be intentional with being a peacemaker among Christians of other races?

Count it all joy, my brothers, when you meet trials of various kinds, for you know that the testing of your faith produces steadfastness. And let steadfastness have its full effect, that you may be perfect and complete, lacking in nothing.

James 1:2-4

All our difficulties are only platforms for the manifestations of God's grace, power and love.

Hudson Taylor

19

PAINFUL JOY

I CAN STILL REMEMBER THOSE EARLY DAYS of weight training when I was a teenager. I would be *so* sore afterwards, especially during times when I increased the amount of weight I was lifting. The reason my muscles hurt after those sessions was because the muscle fibers had experienced microscopic trauma and my body was working hard to repair and rebuild them to be stronger than before. The pain wasn't actually from the tiny tears; rather it was a side effect of the muscle strengthening process.

Life is a lot like that. You and I will have seasons in this exile that are truly painful. Trials, suffering, burdens, heartbreak – they can all wear us down and tear us apart. When we go through these experiences it feels like God has added some weight to the bar of life. At times we don't feel like we can go on, that we don't have the strength to make it through. Yet, somehow, we do make it through and almost always we can look back and see how the Lord grew us through those grueling days.

In the first chapter of his letter, James writes that the Christian pilgrim ought to view adversity in this life differently than those who do not know God. He writes, *"Count it all joy, my brothers, when you meet trials of various kinds"* (James 1:2). James says "exceeding joy" or "abundant delight" should be our disposition toward life's difficulties. I know it sounds crazy. You're wondering, "was James a masochist?" No, he wasn't interested in experiencing pain for pain's sake; rather, he had confidence in two things: 1) God is in control of every aspect of our lives, and 2) God is using every experience in our lives, even our trials, to mold us more into the image of Christ.

You and I work out to grow our physical strength and endurance. Our Heavenly Father sends us into the training of trials to produce spiritual and emotional strength and endurance – *"for you know that the testing of your faith produces steadfastness. And let steadfastness have its full effect, that you may be perfect and complete, lacking in nothing"* (James 1:3-4). The word "testing" in this passage is connected to the refining process that gold and silver go through to create a purer metal. Likewise, the Christian's sufferings are a crucible that refines away the impurities of our sin and weakness, making us more completely like our Savior. Peter wrote something similar: *"you have been grieved by various trials, so that the tested genuineness of your faith—more precious than gold that perishes though it is tested by fire—may be found to result in praise and glory and honor at the revelation of Jesus Christ"* (1 Peter 1:6-7). Adversity leads to adoration; our problems and pain become our praise.

Many of you are in the midst of some difficulty right now – a wayward child, financial struggle, relational conflict, sickness, the loss of someone you love. I know these words may not be easy to receive if you are experiencing much pain and sorrow. However, I know the Lord loves you and is trustworthy. Continually turn to him in this fire. And, though it is difficult, keep your eyes set on things beyond this world, *"for this light momentary affliction is preparing for us an eternal weight of glory beyond all comparison"* (2 Corinthians 4:17).

PRAYER

Father, life can be hard at times. I need your help to view my struggles through the lens of your sovereignty and love. May you grant me the faith to have joy through my trials because I really do believe you're doing something through them, even when I can't see it. For your glory, may you use my adversity to declare your grace, power, and love to the world. Amen.

PONDER

1. How has God proven himself faithful through the trials you have faced?
2. Looking back at your more recent trials, in what ways was Christian maturity produced in you in greater degrees?
3. Do you have any friends who are experiencing hardship right now? Pray James 1:2-4 over them.

But I say to you who hear, love your
enemies, do good to those who hate
you, bless those who curse you,
pray for those who abuse you.

Luke 6:27-28

Returning hate for hate multiplies hate,
adding deeper darkness to a night already
devoid of stars. Darkness cannot drive out
darkness; only light can do that. Hate cannot
drive out hate; only love can do that.

Martin Luther King, Jr.

20

LOVE 'EM

IN 401 A.D. A TEENAGE BOY BY THE NAME OF PATRICK was kidnapped by pirates from the coastline of Britannia and brought to the pagan isle of Ireland. There Patrick was enslaved to a family of sheep herders and immersed in a culture of witchcraft, spells, and spirits. His captivity was very difficult, to say the least. However, over time, Patrick began to see that God was using this great trial to draw him closer to Jesus. As Patrick spent considerable time in prayer and devotion, he began to develop love instead of hate for his captors and a desire to serve them better.

After six years of captivity, at the age of 22, Patrick was able to flee his captors and return to Britannia. Yet in the ensuing years, Patrick's Christ-centered concern for the pagan Irish people would continue to grow. Eventually, he would train for Christian service and make the choice to return to Ireland as a missionary. God so greatly used Patrick over his thirty years of ministry that he is credited with evangelizing most of Ireland. Today, people all over the world wear green in his honor each March.

Because Patrick chose love in the face of hate, many were brought to a saving knowledge of Jesus Christ. He embodied the words of Jesus in Luke 6:27-28 – *"Love your enemies, do good to those who hate you, bless those who curse you, pray for those who abuse you."* We may never be kidnapped and brought to a foreign land, but most of us will experience varying levels of hatefulness and hostility in our lives. However, since we bear the name of Christ, the Lord calls us to a different response to hatred than the world typically demonstrates. Like Patrick, we are to love, do good, bless, and pray for those who hate, curse, and abuse us.

Love Your Enemies

The Greek word used here for "love" is *agape*. Some have described this kind of love as "unconditional," and that's definitely the case in our calling to love our enemies. We do not love our enemies on the condition that they stop opposing us. No, we love them in the midst of their white-hot anger directed our way. Why would God call us to do something that seems to fly in the face of conventional wisdom? Why would he command Christians to show favor to those who so deeply oppose them? Because that is what Jesus has done for each one of us; he loved us to the uttermost in the face of our hate. Colossians 1:21-22 reads, *"Once you were alienated from God and were enemies in your minds because of your evil behavior. But now he has reconciled you by Christ's physical body through death to present you holy in his sight, without blemish and free from accusation."* By the power of the Spirit of Christ who dwells in us we can love our enemies!

Do Good To Those Who Hate You/Bless Those Who Curse You

The reason we bless those who curse us is not because God wants us to be "nice." Yes, we are called to express the spiritual fruit of kindness. However, the ultimate purpose of returning love for hate is that God would be glorified. Consider this verse: *"In the same way, let your light shine before others, so that they may see your good works and give glory to your Father who is in heaven"* (Matthew 5:16). When our greatest aim in life is God's glory, we are freed to express love in the most courageous of ways to the most undeserving of people.

Pray For Those Who Abuse You

If we are ever to love our enemies and do good to those who hate us, we must first be willing to pray for them. When we pray for those who abuse us, we see them as human beings created in God's image, for whom Christ died. In prayer, we are brought into the presence of our merciful King who leads us to pray that we would be forgiven as we forgive others. In prayer, we are reminded of how patient the Lord has been with us and his desire for all people to come to repentance. Prayer has a way of shaping our hearts more into the mold of Christ and leading us to join the Father's work of drawing people to the Son.

PRAYER

Lord Jesus, we really must rely upon your strength when it comes to loving those who mistreat us and malign our names. I naturally want to defend myself and fight back against those who sin against me. Help me to reject hatred toward my enemies and transform my heart that I may even be favorable toward them, actively choosing to bless them and pray for them. For your glory, my King. Amen.

PONDER

1. Spend some time thinking about what Jesus did for you through his life, death, and resurrection even when he knew you would be aligned against him: *"but God shows his love for us in that while we were still sinners, Christ died for us"* (Romans 5:8).
2. Which part of the Christlike response to hatred is most difficult for you – loving, doing good, blessing, or serving?
3. Think about who most opposes you. Maybe it is a particular person or a group of people. Ask the Lord for wisdom on how you might actively bless them today.

Then Mordecai told them to reply to Esther, "Do not think to yourself that in the king's palace you will escape any more than all the other Jews. For if you keep silent at this time, relief and deliverance will rise for the Jews from another place, but you and your father's house will perish. And who knows whether you have not come to the kingdom for such a time as this?" Then Esther told them to reply to Mordecai, "Go, gather all the Jews to be found in Susa, and hold a fast on my behalf, and do not eat or drink for three days, night or day. I and my young women will also fast as you do. Then I will go to the king, though it is against the law, and if I perish, I perish."

Esther 4:13-16

Open your mouth for the mute,
for the rights of all who are destitute.
Open your mouth, judge righteously,
defend the rights of the poor and needy

Proverbs 31:8-9

21

SPEAK UP!

THE BOOK OF ESTHER TELLS THE STORY of a courageous young woman living in exile who used her influence to bring deliverance to God's people. Esther was a Jew born in exile in Persia. When she was a teenager, King Xerxes (486-465 B.C.) ordered that the most beautiful young women throughout his empire be brought to him that he might choose a new queen. Unfortunately, this was no glorified beauty pageant. These young women, who were viewed as property, would be stripped from their families and communities to live near the palace at the behest of the king. Esther, who lived in the capital city of Susa and had been raised by her cousin Mordecai, was one of the young women brought to the king's harem. The Bible tells us that Esther "had a beautiful figure and was lovely to look at" (Esther 2:7). Eventually, she won the favor of Xerxes and became his queen. However, Xerxes did not know that she was a Jew.

Esther's relative Mordecai appears to have been a leader of the Jewish community who was involved in the affairs of the state. At a certain point after she had become queen, Mordecai informed Esther that a man by the name of Haman was plotting to bring destruction upon the Jewish people living in Persia. Mordecai asked Esther to intervene and use her God-given position to speak up for them. Esther's response to Mordecai demonstrates her courage and trust in the Lord, *"Go, gather all the Jews to be found in Susa, and hold a fast on my behalf, and do not eat or drink for three days, night or day. I and my young women will also fast as you do. Then I will go to the king, though it is against the law, and if I perish, I perish"* (Esther 4:16). Through a series of events, the Lord revealed his sovereign hand in the lives of Esther and Mordecai, bringing about the deliverance of the Jews and Haman's destruction.

We can learn more from Esther's story than we might first realize. Like Esther, we live in a state of exile (hers was physical, ours is spiritual). Like Esther, we live in a time of injustice in which God call us to speak up for the vulnerable. Like Esther, we require courage to be an advocate. Like Esther, we serve a God who desires that we demonstrate faith. Like Esther, we serve a faithful God who is with his people, intervening in the lives of the needy through their courage.

Which groups need "Esthers" today? The list is long, but I'll note three.

Children (Unborn/Orphans/Trafficking Victims)

No group has been so historically marginalized as children. Jesus was revolutionary in the ways he spent time with children and invited them into his presence. Today, there is still great need for advocacy for children – especially the unborn, orphans, and those who are victims of human trafficking. James wrote that to care for such vulnerable groups is "pure and undefiled religion" (James 1:27). And, thankfully, there are many ways to be involved – fostering, adoption, respite care, advocating, serving a local pregnancy center, giving to an anti-trafficking ministry. May we be willing to open our mouths and open our lives that these dear children may be loved with the love of Christ.

The Poor

The Bible is replete with verses calling God's people to show honor and kindness to the poor. Consider just two: 1) Proverbs 14:31 – *"Whoever oppresses a poor man insults his Maker, but he who is generous to the needy honors him."* 2) Proverbs 29:7 – *"A righteous man knows the rights of the poor; a wicked man does not understand such knowledge."* Oftentimes in societies the poor are forgotten, neglected, and marginalized. The Lord's desire is that we would love our poor neighbors as ourselves. As our spiritual, physical, and relational needs are met, we should seek to meet those needs in their lives as well through a variety of ministries: food pantries, Bible studies, medical clinics, legal counsel, financial advice, educational and job opportunities.

Immigrants

Sometimes the poor among us today are immigrants. Old Testament law was exceptionally favorable toward the non-natives that dwelt within Israel. Leviticus 19:34 reads, *"You shall treat the stranger who sojourns with you as the native among you, and you shall love him as yourself, for you were strangers in the land of Egypt: I am the LORD your God."* This encouragement from Leviticus is a far cry from some of the rhetoric that we hear today. Though it is true that our nation should have effective immigration laws and enforcement of those laws, the primary responsibility of Christians is to show hospitality to international students, refugees, and others who have entered our communities from beyond our nation's borders.

PRAYER

Father, may I have courage to use my influence and speak up for others. May I not be primarily concerned with how I might be affected by the consequences of my advocacy. May I be first moved by your compassion for the vulnerable and your desire for justice. Show me how to "defend the rights of the poor and needy." Amen.

PONDER

1. Though God's name is never explicitly mentioned in the Book of Esther, his providence is clearly evidenced. How so?
2. What about Esther's story most inspires you?
3. Which vulnerable group are you most led to advocate for?

And when evening came, the boat was out on the sea, and he was alone on the land. And he saw that they were making headway painfully, for the wind was against them. And about the fourth watch of the night he came to them, walking on the sea. He meant to pass by them, but when they saw him walking on the sea they thought it was a ghost, and cried out, for they all saw him and were terrified. But immediately he spoke to them and said, "Take heart; it is I. Do not be afraid." And he got into the boat with them, and the wind ceased.

Mark 6:47-51

In the world you will have tribulation. But take heart; I have overcome the world.

John 16:33

22

LIFE IS A...

M ANY ARE FAMILIAR WITH THE WELL-LOVED 1994 film *Forrest Gump* and the memorable line uttered by its title character played by Tom Hanks – "Life is like a box of chocolates, you never know what you're gonna get." As the movie depicted, Forrest knew firsthand that life could bring both joy and pain. Others have described life in different ways. Tom Cochrane, and later Rascal Flatts, would sing, "Life is a highway." Muhammed Ali said, "Life is a gamble." For so many in this world, life is a struggle; not necessarily a joyless struggle, but a battle nonetheless. We age. We have to pay bills. Our children don't always obey. Christians living as exiles in this world sometimes face additional challenges as they seek to be faithful. Thankfully, we have the Spirit of Christ as a Helper in the fight.

In Mark 6:45-52 we see the disciples in a struggle to survive. As they were making their way across the Sea of Galilee, a storm began to brew that threatened their lives. No doubt fear and anxiety began to set in as they wondered where Jesus was in the midst of this storm. In this account, Mark shares with his readers three truths that encourage them (and us) in our struggle.

Jesus Sees Us In The Struggle

In Jesus' day, it would normally take about six hours to cross the Sea of Galilee by boat. However, the disciples had now been on the lake for over eight hours and they were nowhere near the shore. As one version says, they were "straining at the oars."

Though Jesus was alone on the land, he was not unaware of the great challenges his disciples were facing (Mark 6:47-48). No doubt, he had compassion on them in their struggle.

As we face our own storms, we can often wonder whether anybody sees us, especially God. Does he see what I'm dealing with? Does he even care? A verse to remember in those times is Matthew 10:30-31 – *"But even the hairs of your head are all numbered. Fear not, therefore; you are of more value than many sparrows."* Not only does Jesus see you, but he is aware of the even the smallest details of your life. He knows this because you are of such worth to him.

Jesus Shows Us His Glory In The Struggle

The text says with little fanfare, *"And about the fourth watch of the night he came to them, walking on the sea"* (Mark 6:48). For us who've heard this story many times, the power of these words can be lost, but for the disciples in those early morning hours, this was no casual occurrence. A man was walking on water. Jesus was showing himself to be Lord of the sea, able to tame this wild place that brought great fear to ancient minds. Mark goes on to say that Jesus meant to pass by them. At first this seems strange – why would Jesus intend to pass them up? But then we remember how the Lord revealed himself to Moses and Elijah in the Old Testament. He passed by them. Jesus wanted to show the disciples something of his glory. He had to pass before them in the pain of their struggle so they could see his power.

The way God reveals himself in our struggle may not look the way we want, and it doesn't usually happen according to our timing. But as we look back upon those seasons of time, we have greater vision to see how the Lord was showing more of his person, provision, and presence to us.

Jesus in With Us In The Struggle

Before Jesus ever gets into the boat with the disciples, he

knows something that would seem to disqualify them from his presence: their faith is small and their hearts are hard. The text says they were "utterly astounded," "they did not understand," and "their hearts were hard." No doubt, each of us on the worst days of our struggle are like the disciples – lacking in faith, a little hard of heart. And we think this repels Jesus, that it pushes him away. But Jesus never denies his own. In fact, when Jesus sees us hurting in the struggle, he is even more compelled to come and offer us his mercy and grace. That's when Jesus gets in the boat with us. For Christians, his Spirit is always with us, but there is an added measure of his Spirit's comfort when we need it most.

Life is a struggle, but Jesus is with us. Life is a struggle, but Jesus is able.

PRAYER

Jesus, it brings me comfort to know that you see me, are with me, and desire to use my struggle to lead me to know you more deeply. Help me to trust you, especially when it feels like I'm straining at the oars in the early morning hours. Give me eyes to see you as you pass before me and come sit beside me. Amen.

PONDER

1. Which of the three truths about Jesus from this passage brings you the most encouragement? Why?
2. What area of your life would you most describe as a struggle?
3. If you know someone who is experiencing significant difficulty, pray they may know the presence of Christ with them and consider how you could encourage them with your words or actions.

For we know that if the tent that is our earthly home is destroyed, we have a building from God, a house not made with hands, eternal in the heavens. For in this tent we groan, longing to put on our heavenly dwelling, if indeed by putting it on we may not be found naked. For while we are still in this tent, we groan, being burdened—not that we would be unclothed, but that we would be further clothed, so that what is mortal may be swallowed up by life. He who has prepared us for this very thing is God, who has given us the Spirit as a guarantee.

2 Corinthians 5:1-5

So is it with the resurrection of the dead. What is sown is perishable; what is raised is imperishable. It is sown in dishonor; it is raised in glory. It is sown in weakness; it is raised in power. It is sown a natural body; it is raised a spiritual body. If there is a natural body, there is also a spiritual body.

1 Corinthians 15:40-44

23

GLAMPING

L IFE ON EARTH IN THIS BODY can be difficult at times. Disease, weakness, infertility, injury, pain, and psychological disorders can all plague the body. Children are born with birth defects. Cancer diagnoses increase among our friends as we age. This body, like the rest of creation, is marred by brokenness. Every part of it breaks down over time if it is not already significantly broken to begin with. Then, one day, our heart stops beating, we breathe our last, and physical death comes upon us.

However, death does not have the last word. It is not the last act. It is rather the end of Act I before the intermission and the beginning of the more climactic Act II. The end of this life is merely a transition. And what awaits the believer is in many respects incomprehensibly joyous. There are not words to fully capture the experience the redeemed will have when they receive their resurrected bodies.

Part of what helps us through our experience in these earthly bodies is the confidence that there is so much prepared for us in the restored creation in the new heavens and new earth. In 2 Corinthians 5:1-5, Paul encourages the believers in Corinth with some truths regarding the resurrected bodies they will receive in the life to come. May these two truths strengthen us through our sojourning as strangers on this journey.

From a Tent to a Building

Have you ever slept in a tent? It's kind of fun for a night or two, but then you start thinking about your pillowtop bed in your insulated home and you realize that one is better than the other. Paul says we've been given a temporary bodily home on this earth that is like a "tent" (2 Corinthians 5:1). Tents are functional, but limited. This body that we have during our earthly exile is like that. And it makes sense, for exiles throughout time have often lived in temporary dwellings like tents. However, in glory, Christians will receive an eternal, heavenly "house" of a body that God has specially designed.

These new resurrected bodies are described as imperishable, glorious, and powerful (1 Corinthians 15:42-44). I could be way off on this, but I believe the superhero movies our kids love to watch only scratch the surface of the kind of experience we will have in our resurrected bodies. Philippians 3:21 says Jesus *"will transform our lowly body to be like his glorious body"* (Philippians 3:21). Will we be able to fly? I sure hope so!

Longing For More

While we await our new bodies on the other side, we exile here realizing that our true home and life are not yet manifest. Thus, Paul writes, *"we groan, longing to put on our heavenly dwelling"* (2 Corinthians 5:2). Groaning, longing – these are part of the normal experience of the Christian exile. We desire more than this life and this body can offer. In fact, that desire is part of the work of God who has given us his Holy Spirit as a guarantee of the things to come (2 Corinthians 5:5). The word *guarantee* in the Greek is a financial term that means "deposit, down payment, or earnest money." By giving us the Spirit, the Lord is proving that though we are not yet with him glory, we have not been left as orphans in this exile. Even today we have access to God's life-transforming power.

PRAYER

Father, you are so amazing! It is incredible to think that one day you will give us bodies like our resurrected Lord's. That's so cool! Knowing that this earthly body is only temporary, may I not grow too discouraged when it fails. Help me set my eyes on the promise that you have prepared a new body for me "eternal in the heavens." Amen.

PONDER

1. How does the "deposit/guarantee" of the Holy Spirit help us to keep our focus on the life to come?
2. What truth from 2 Corinthians 5:1-5 or 1 Corinthians 15:40-44 about the resurrected body do you find most amazing?
3. If these bodies are going to wear out, should we care for them? The Bible answers in the affirmative. However, what might stewardship of our bodies look like in a culture that is simultaneously gluttonous and overly body-conscious?

All this is from God, who through Christ reconciled us to himself and gave us the ministry of reconciliation; that is, in Christ God was reconciling the world to himself, not counting their trespasses against them, and entrusting to us the message of reconciliation. Therefore, we are ambassadors for Christ, God making his appeal through us. We implore you on behalf of Christ, be reconciled to God.

2 Corinthians 5:18-20

It is the duty of every Christian to be Christ to his neighbor.

Martin Luther

24

AMBASSADORS

THOUGH BENJAMIN FRANKLIN NEVER SERVED AS PRESIDENT of the United States, he held a role prior to the forming of our Union that was just as important: he was chosen to be the Thirteen Colonies' ambassador to France. The Colonies were in great need of money and supplies if they were to secure their independence from Britain, and France was the one nation that could help them gain victory. For almost two years, Franklin worked tirelessly to secure aid and support for the revolution. Many historians believe that France's support was essential to our triumph over British forces.

Being an ambassador isn't easy work. You usually live away from your home among a people who may or may not appreciate your presence. Sometimes the place where you live is hostile or at least antagonistic toward the desires of the government you represent. And yet, being an ambassador is one of the highest callings one could receive. As an ambassador you are the primary representative and messenger of another realm.

In 2 Corinthians 5:20, the Apostle Paul wrote that he was (and we are) "ambassadors for Christ." We are kingdom citizens living on earth as representatives of Christ and his reign. As his ambassadors we not only represent his ways, but we also bring a "message of reconciliation" to those who dwell on earth (2 Corinthians 5:19). This Good News is a proclamation that sinful humanity may be reconciled with God because Jesus has secured forgiveness through his death on a cross. As Paul declares, "*in*

Christ God was reconciling the world to himself, not counting their trespasses against them" (2 Corinthians 5:19). This message began with Jesus and then was given to the Twelve following his resurrection. Over the past two thousand years it has been extended to disciples of Christ across the generations and throughout the nations. Today, the message of reconciliation is entrusted to us.

As you consider this passage, you might feel a little overwhelmed by the significance of this task and calling. Maybe a little like Frodo Baggins in *The Lord of the Rings* – "I'm just a Hobbit. I'm not really sure I want this task. The shire is mighty fine and Mordor is a pretty scary place." I totally get it! Our role as Christ's ambassadors can feel daunting. But here's the thing – we're far more than Hobbits. We are Spirit-filled sons and daughters of the Most High King who have been set free by this message of reconciliation and enabled by God's grace to represent him to others through word and deed.

So, how does one even begin living as an ambassador? Good question. Start by "living your faith publicly," says pastor Tim Keller. Too many Christians either live privatized lives (not open to sharing their faith) or secluded lives (having no non-Christian friends). Public Christians, on the other hand, don't let fear, pride, pessimism, or indifference hold them back from sharing their faith. In addition, they choose to welcome others into their lives who may not have a relationship with Jesus yet.

As you seek to be intentional as an ambassador of Christ and messenger of reconciliation with a friend, here are some steps to consider:

1. Let the person know you are a Christian.
2. Listen to their joys and problems.
3. Be transparent – share your life, too.
4. Pray for them.
5. Ask about their beliefs.
6. Share your own faith journey.
7. Invite them to church functions.

8. Share God's Word.
9. Share the gospel.

PRAYER

Jesus, I want to faithfully represent you and the gospel. I want to be an ambassador who looks and sounds like my King. I praise you for reconciling me to the Father. Help me to implore others to be reconciled as well. May I embrace the fact that you are making your appeal to the world through me. Grant me courage in this calling and responsibility. Amen.

PONDER

1. How do you feel about the fact that God would choose to make his appeal to lost people through you?
2. Who implored you to be reconciled to God? (That is, who led you to Jesus?)
4. What most holds you back from being a "public Christian" who is an intentional ambassador for Christ?

Now when they heard these things they were enraged, and they ground their teeth at him. But he, full of the Holy Spirit, gazed into heaven and saw the glory of God, and Jesus standing at the right hand of God… Then they cast him out of the city and stoned him… And Saul approved of his execution. And there arose on that day a great persecution against the church in Jerusalem, and they were all scattered throughout the regions of Judea and Samaria, except the apostles … But Saul was ravaging the church, and entering house after house, he dragged off men and women and committed them to prison. Now those who were scattered went about preaching the word.

Acts 7:54-55, 58; 8:1, 3-4

He is no fool who gives what he cannot keep to gain that which he cannot lose.

Jim Elliot

25

PERSECUTED, NOT FORSAKEN

I N 2015 ATLANTA FIRE CHIEF KELVIN COCHRANE, a 34-year veteran of the department, was fired. Chief Cochrane wasn't fired due to dereliction of duty or misuse of public funds, he was terminated because of a Bible study he wrote – a study that took a biblical position on matters such as cohabitation and homosexuality. Cochrane was suspended for "discrimination" and then ultimately released. Unfortunately, Kelvin Cochrane's case is not an isolated one. Christians are increasingly being pressured to keep their mouths shut about their beliefs and are threatened with demotion, termination, or lawsuits if they choose otherwise. On our school campuses, Christian students often face ridicule if they choose to publicly identify as a follower of Jesus and especially if they uphold traditional sexual values.

There is no doubt that persecution is on the rise in the United States. Some may say, "Isn't that a little strong? No one is being killed." It might help to have an appropriate definition of persecution. Persecution is "hostility and ill-treatment because of religious beliefs." Most persecution around the world doesn't involve imprisonment or death. It looks like rejection and marginalization, then at times reduction of rights. As our culture drifts further and further away from biblical norms, our position as spiritual exiles in America will increasingly lead us to experience the truth of Paul's words—"*Indeed, all who desire to live a godly life in Christ Jesus will be persecuted*" (2 Timothy 3:12).

In Acts 7-8 we see persecution carried out to its fullest

lengths as Stephen, one of the earliest leaders in the Church, is stoned for testifying of Christ. The account recorded by Luke demonstrates three truths evident in persecution that will encourage us in our struggle.

Persecution Results From Hostility To Jesus

The first truth is persecution results from hostility to Jesus. Luke records the crowds being so enraged at what Stephen had said that they *"ground their teeth at him"* (Acts 7:54). What had Stephen said that was so blasphemous? He had declared that Jesus was the long-prophesied Messiah who was greater that Moses and David. Stephen's testimony was a threat to the very heart of the Jewish religious elite. Their authority was based upon their position to interpret the Mosaic code and identify the Davidic Messiah to come. Jesus demolished that authority.

Whatever the "thing" is that the culture worships, whenever it is threatened by Jesus, persecution is close by. In ancient Rome it was the Empire; in China it is the Communist Party; in Muslim nations it is the Koran and Muhammed; in the United States it is unfettered sexual freedom. We often think that persecution exists because people don't like Christians. And, though that may be true, hostility doesn't begin with us. It starts with Jesus. *"If the world hates you, know that it has hated me before it hated you"* (John 15:18).

Persecution Leads To Intimacy With Christ

The second truth is persecution leads to intimacy with Christ. Acts 7:55 records that Stephen *"full of the Holy Spirit, gazed into heaven and saw the glory of God, and Jesus standing at the right hand of God."* In the darkest moments of his persecution, Stephen had a vision of the risen Lord. Jesus looking down on his servant seems to be communicating, "I see you, Stephen, and I am with you." If you were to speak with the persecuted, they would tell you the same thing, *"If you are insulted for the name of Christ, you are blessed, because the Spirit of glory and of God rests upon you"* (1 Peter 4:14).

Persecution Creates Opportunity For Ministry

The third truth is persecution creates opportunity for ministry. There are two examples of this in our passage from Acts 7-8. The first involves the scattering of those who were persecuted and their preaching of the Word of God (Acts 8:4). In fact, some of those who were scattered made their way to Antioch and helped birth the most missional of the early churches (Acts 11:19). The second example is that of Saul, the persecutor of the Church who witnessed Stephen's stoning and later would be known primarily as Paul the apostle. No doubt, Paul saw something in Stephen that he had never seen before – a deep and abiding intimacy with God. Our persecution can lead our persecutors to see the power of the gospel firsthand, as Paul went on to mention in Philippians 1:12-14.

PRAYER

Lord, no one wants to walk through the fires of persecution, including me. Yet, I see in your Word that you use all things, even hostility against me and hatred of your Name. Grant me the courage I need to stand for you. Help me be bold like Stephen, that you may lead more Pauls to faith in the gospel of Jesus Christ. Amen.

PONDER

1. How does Jesus standing in honor of Stephen's courage encourage you to be faithful to our Savior?
2. What leads some people to have boldness in the face of persecution and others to shrink away?
3. How can Christians better prepare themselves to be bold in the face of opposition?

Do you not know that in a race all the runners run, but only one receives the prize? So run that you may obtain it. Every athlete exercises self-control in all things. They do it to receive a perishable wreath, but we an imperishable. So I do not run aimlessly; I do not box as one beating the air. But I discipline my body and keep it under control, lest after preaching to others I myself should be disqualified.

1 Corinthians 9:24-27

No soldier gets entangled in civilian pursuits, since his aim is to please the one who enlisted him. An athlete is not crowned unless he competes according to the rules. It is the hard-working farmer who ought to have the first share of the crops.

2 Timothy 2:4-6

26

26.2

Y OU EITHER HAVE ONE OR YOU SMIRK AS YOU DRIVE past them—
the 13.1 and 26.2 stickers on the backs of Honda Odysseys
and Subaru Outbacks. These modern-day trophies for stay-at-
home moms and weekend warriors are part of our *nouveau*
bumper sticker culture. Regardless of your thoughts about the
stickers, few would question the amount of dedication required
to actually run a marathon. For most people it involves months
of physical training, a significant diet adjustment, and even a
reorientation of one's schedule. Running a race of that magni-
tude requires laser-like focus.

In his first letter to the church in Corinth, Paul wrote that
Christians should view their lives as a race run for the sake of the
gospel. Disciples of Christ should be like Olympic athletes whose
dedication is unquestioned and whose focus is on nothing short
of the gold. Paul's use of this metaphor in 1 Corinthians 9 and
then again in 2 Timothy 2 is employed because the apostle knew
how easily we can get distracted by the things of this world. As
resident aliens living in foreign territory, we need to keep our
eyes set on kingdom business and give all our energies to it. To
encourage his Corinthian readers, Paul offered three driving ideas to invigorate their running of this race.

Determination

First, we are to run with determination. Paul said, *"So run
that you may obtain [the prize]"* (1 Corinthians 9:24). The prize for

believers is the "imperishable wreath" of their homegoing to be with the Lord when they die. Paul was saying to put all you can into the knowledge that you will receive that prize. For some Christians their "race" may be a few short years, but for most they will be running for decades. As avid runners will tell you the lengthier races require a higher level of grit and perseverance due to both internal and external factors. It's the same in the life of the disciple. We have to fight off sin internally and press through obstacles the world throws at us.

Direction

Second, we are to run with direction. We are not to run aimlessly but with a particular purpose and trajectory. Someone once said, "start with the end in mind." As Christians we know that one day we will be standing inches away from the resurrected Lord, looking into his face as he welcomes us into our heavenly home. In that moment we are going to fully realize that the only thing that really mattered in this life was what we did for the gospel and the kingdom. So, Paul is saying with that in mind, live your life accordingly. The goal of our life should be Christ glorified – in us, by our neighbors, and among the nations.

Discipline

Third, we are to run with discipline. Continuing his running metaphor, Paul wrote, *"Every athlete exercises self-control in all things"* (1 Corinthians 9:25) and *"I discipline my body and keep it under control"* (1 Corinthians 9:27). Paul was consciously aware that the one thing that could most disqualify him from the race, the one thing that could most strip him of the greatest experience of his prize, was the flesh. It is the same for us. We must continually place the flesh under the control of the Holy Spirit. To do this we need to see the Spirit of God as our spiritual life and fitness coach. He provides us with a plan for spiritual nourishment, reminding us to avoid "junk food." He also pushes us hard in the weight room of spiritual growth, putting us through all kinds of exercises that build our spiritual muscles so we may run the race with greater perseverance.

Here's the plan I've seen work for just about every spiritual athlete:

Nutrition: The Word, Prayer, Worship, Community
Training: Service, Evangelism, Giving, Suffering

PRAYER

Father, I want to run my race with determination, direction, and discipline like an athlete crossing the finish line with chest out, not in pride but pressing hard through the last step. I need your Spirit to train me to run harder after the gospel. I need his help to have self-control to lay aside every weight that bears me down and to put off the sin that so easily entangles my feet, that my race may be run for the glory of Jesus Christ. Amen.

PONDER

1. How did Jesus embody the metaphor of a persevering athlete, especially in his last days?
2. Are you an athlete? If so, how does this metaphor encourage you? If you do not consider yourself an athlete, what is something in your life that requires determination, direction, and discipline?
3. What area of your life is most in need of Spirit-empowered self-control?

And they came and said to him, "Teacher, we know that you are true and do not care about anyone's opinion. For you are not swayed by appearances, but truly teach the way of God. Is it lawful to pay taxes to Caesar, or not? Should we pay them, or should we not?" But, knowing their hypocrisy, he said to them, "Why put me to the test? Bring me a denarius and let me look at it." And they brought one. And he said to them, "Whose likeness and inscription is this?" They said to him, "Caesar's." Jesus said to them, "Render to Caesar the things that are Caesar's, and to God the things that are God's." And they marveled at him.

Mark 12:14-17

Let every person be subject to the governing authorities. For there is no authority except from God, and those that exist have been instituted by God.

Romans 13:1

27

RENDER UNTO CAESAR

S INCE 1972 GALLUP HAS CONDUCTED a "Trust in Government" poll of Americans. In its first poll it found that the percentage of respondents who had a "Great Deal" or "Fair Amount" of faith in the Executive Branch and Legislative Branch was 73% and 71%, respectively. By 2020, those numbers had plummeted to 43% and 33%, respectively. Trust in American institutions, and especially the federal government, is as low as it has ever been.

Though we see growing mistrust of government in our own day, it doesn't come close to the feelings and actions of the Jewish people toward Imperial Rome during Jesus' day. By the time Jesus was born, the Jews had already been under Roman subjection for over sixty years. This domination by foreign leaders was viewed by many in Israel as an affront to the sovereignty of God. So much so that insurrections were not uncommon and whole parties, like the Zealots, were committed to the overthrow of their Roman oppressors.

On a certain occasion the Jewish religious leaders sought to use the question of loyalty to Rome to trap Jesus. They asked him whether it was morally correct (in line with the Law of God) to pay taxes to Caesar. The Pharisees and Herodians were hoping to get Jesus in trouble with either the crowds (if he answered in the affirmative) or the Roman authorities (if he answered negatively). However, Jesus' answer stunned them. He said, *"Render to Caesar the things that are Caesar's, and to God the things that are God's"* (Mark 12:17). Jesus was saying that Rome had a certain kind of authority and God had another; they were not the same. By stating his answer in this way, Jesus was denying the deification of the Emperor and the State, but he was also rejecting the idea of an essential Jewish theocracy.

Jesus' words not only directed the Jews to better understand a godly approach to their relationship with Imperial Rome, but they help Christians discern what our posture toward the civil authorities should be in light of the fact that we are citizens of another kingdom. In short: we should yield to our governing authorities in matters for which they have been granted power and responsibility. And, in this life, those governing us have been granted much authority by God. Paul writes, *"Therefore whoever resists the authorities resists what God has appointed, and those who resist will incur judgment"* (Romans 13:2). Likewise, Peter declared, *"Be subject for the Lord's sake to every human institution, whether it be to the emperor as supreme, or the governors sent by him to punish those who do evil and praise those who do good"* (1 Peter 2:13-14).

The anti-government streak that is alive and well today in our society is not driven by the Spirit of God. For if Jesus and Paul and Peter could tell their hearers who lived under totalitarian regimes that they should obey their leaders under the vast majority of circumstances, then we who live in free, democratic societies in which Christians can both vote for their representatives and serve as those representatives should be even more willing to be subject to them. This doesn't mean that we should necessarily agree with all of our leaders' decisions or that we should support their policies uncritically. However, it does mean that once we have done everything in our power to support a specific position, policy, or candidate that we believe more greatly approximates the values of the kingdom of God, we should rest in the sovereignty of God and seek to honor our elected and appointed officials.

Here's a good biblical recipe for a Christian's responsibility to their governmental leaders:

Pray for them (1 Timothy 2:1-3).
Honor them (Romans 13:7).
Submit to them (Titus 3:1).
Serve them (1 Peter 2:16).

PRAYER

Father, all authority derives from you, including the power that resides in the halls of government. Teach me to show more honor and respect to those you have placed in positions of civil authority. Grant me peace when my candidate is on the losing end of the ballot or when my party is no longer in power. May my hope for change in this world be ever set upon you and never upon a politician. In all of this I pray that you would be glorified as the King of Kings. Amen.

PONDER

1. Why do you think God calls his people to be subject to their governmental authorities – whether they are dictators like Caesar or duly elected leaders like the President of the United States?
2. Which of the Bible verses referenced in this study most shocked you the first time you read them? Why?
3. How do you need to be more "Christian" in your approach to government?

If then you have been raised with Christ,
seek the things that are above, where Christ
is, seated at the right hand of God. Set your
minds on things that are above, not on things
that are on earth. For you have died, and your
life is hidden with Christ in God.

Colossians 3:1-3

Apart from a Christian mind we will either
be taken captive by the myriad of worldviews
contending for our attention, or we will
fail to make the Christian voice heard
and considered above the din.

James Emery White

28

SO HEAVENLY MINDED

YOU MAY BE FAMILIAR WITH THE QUOTE, "Don't be so heavenly-minded that you're no earthly good." Though I understand the intention behind the statement – that we would be engaged in the world – I find it to be contrary to good doctrine. In fact, I believe the opposite of the statement to be true – "Be SO heavenly-minded that you might be of earthly good." That's at least what Paul seems to be saying in Colossians 3.

The apostle was writing to a church that was placed in one of the most diverse cities in the Roman Empire. Colossae was religiously diverse, culturally diverse, and philosophically diverse. There were many different people with many different ideas. What concerned Paul was that some of the members of the church in Colossae (the Colossians) were being influenced and led astray by a "hollow and deceptive philosophy" (Colossians 2:8). Kind of sounds like our own day, right? "Hollow and deceptive philosophies" abound in our culture and too often find their ways into our churches as well: humanism (the system of thinking that elevates humans and diminishes God), materialism (the tendency to consider material possessions and physical comfort as being more important than spiritual values), and hedonism (the worship of pleasure – sex, food, entertainment).

Paul's remedy to the Colossian malady was to point them back to Christ and their identity in him – to lead them to be "heavenly-minded." In Colossians 3:1-3, we find two directives to help us reset our eyes upon our true home.

Set Our Hearts On Our Rank In Christ

First, Paul encourages us to set our hearts on our rank in Christ. *"Since then, you have been raised with Christ, set your hearts on things above, where Christ is seated at the right hand of God"* (Colossians 3:1). The apostle wanted his readers to understand that though they were physically on earth, they were spiritually present in heaven with Christ. Being seated with Christ in glory is as much my reality as being seated at my desk as I write this devotional. Christ's resurrection position at the right hand of the Father in the place of honor and position of authority was reserved for the person with the most access to the Sovereign. And you and I sit there with/in Jesus – beloved, entrusted, esteemed, befriended by God. What an amazing truth to behold!

Set Our Minds On Our Reality In Christ

Second, Paul encourages us to set our minds on our reality in Christ. *"Set your minds on things that are above, not on things that are on earth. For you have died, and your life is hidden with Christ in God"* (Colossians 3:2-3). For a second time in this passage Paul mentions "things above." These are unseen things, hidden things that are in heaven where we abide in the risen Lord. We're to put our attention and energy on the fact that we are not of this world. Our minds are to continually turn to our union with Christ and the hidden life. We are to have our thoughts set on the reality that we are no longer characterized by sin because the old self died with Christ and we have been given a new life, empowered from heaven.

So how do we go about setting our hearts and minds on these heavenly realities? It's quite simple:

1. Read the Word.
2. Meditate on the Word.
3. Sing the Word.
4. Memorize the Word.

5. Study the Word
6. Pray the Word.
7. Share the Word.
8. Live the Word.

PRAYER

Father, these truths are almost too great to consider! How can it be that though I am presently living on earth in this body, I am even also residing in your presence in Christ? But you have declared these truths to me and I believe them. May these thoughts soak deep into my mind and penetrate my heart, that I may know you more and experience more of the life you have given me. In all of this may I be of great "earthly good" until you call me to my true home. Amen.

PONDER

1. How does it make you feel that God has so welcomed you into his presence that you sit with Christ at his right hand?
2. In verse 3, Paul says we have died in Christ. What still needs to be put to death in your life today?
3. In what ways is God calling you to "seek the things that are above"?

The God who made the world and everything in it, being Lord of heaven and earth, does not live in temples made by man, nor is he served by human hands, as though he needed anything, since he himself gives to all mankind life and breath and everything. And he made from one man every nation of mankind to live on all the face of the earth, having determined allotted periods and the boundaries of their dwelling place, that they should seek God, and perhaps feel their way toward him and find him. Yet he is actually not far from each one of us.

Acts 17:24-27

Right now, God is working all around you.

Henry Blackaby

29

RIGHT WHERE YOU NEED TO BE

E XILE CAN BE AN UNCOMFORTABLE EXPERIENCE. The fact that we are strangers in this world can lead us to feel like we're fish out of water. If we're not careful, those feelings can lead us to seek respite by continually changing our location, profession, relationships, or the color of paint on our walls. Yet, no change in this world will leave us with any lasting satisfaction because we long for something that is otherworldly. In most cases what we need to do is be faithful to our gospel responsibilities right where God has placed us. We ought to "grow where we've been planted" and to "put down roots" even when the soil is a little harsh.

In Acts 17, we find the Apostle Paul in the Areopagus of Athens speaking to some of the leading thinkers of Greece about the "unknown God" to whom they had built an altar. The summary of Paul's speech to these pagan philosophers bares significant truth regarding God's sovereignty and his care for his creatures. Paul's words, which Luke has recorded, encourage us who sometimes find life in this exile to be difficult and undesirable. Let's consider three declarations of God's providence that speak to his care for us and our calling to missional purposes.

God Has Given Everything You Need

"He himself gives to all mankind life and breath and everything" (Acts 17:25). For those of us who are Christians, we have been given even more (Philippians 4:19). Think about all the Lord has provided you. Start with the most basic of things – a

mind to think, a heart to feel, a body to move, air to breathe, water to drink, food to eat. Then consider how he has blessed you beyond that – family, friends, home, job, health. Now think on those things that are ultimate – salvation, the Holy Spirit, peace, joy, love, faith. He has supplied all our needs as an intentional, devoted Father (Matthew 7:7-11). If there are things you lack (finances, friendship, faith), ask him for them. He cares for you.

God Has Uniquely Placed You In The World

"And he made from one man every nation of mankind to live on all the face of the earth having determined allotted periods and the boundaries of their dwelling place" (Acts 17:26). When and where you were born was no accident. God appointed the exact day and location you would come into the world. He also chose the particular people group you would be born into. He purposed that you would speak a specific language and have a certain culture. He chose all this because you are counted among a *"great multitude that no one could number, from every nation, from all tribes and peoples and languages"* that worship Jesus (Revelation 7:9). Even today, the Lord is lovingly determining the "boundaries of your dwelling place" for the sake of his mission to the nations.

God Wants The People Around You To Know Him

"that they should seek God, and perhaps feel their way toward him and find him. Yet he is actually not far from each one of us" (Acts 17:27). Jesus not only saved you as a worshipper from your people group, but he desires to send you back to your people as an ambassador of the gospel. Just like the woman at the well who went back to her fellow villagers to share the Good News of Christ with them (John 4), God desires that you would speak of him to your neighbors. This is not to say that God will never call you to serve cross-culturally in some way. In fact, today our communities are filled with a great number of diverse people groups. In 2021 (the year in which this book was written), there happen

to be 521 people groups living in the United States, with 97 of them being unreached (less than 2% Christian)!! What an amazing opportunity we have right where God has placed us to be witnesses of the grace and love available in Christ.

I love Henry Blackaby's quote from *Experiencing God*, "Right now, God is working all around you." Do you believe it? We need to be reminded of this often. Don't grow weary or become discouraged. Set your heart on how to join the Lord in the work he is accomplishing right where you are.

PRAYER

Father, help me to be content with where I am today – whether that be where I live or where I work or among the group of people I call friends. Lift up my eyes to see how you are working in these places and among these people, that I my join your Spirit in the work of reconciling the world to you in Christ. Help me to find my satisfaction in you, for you supply my every need. Amen.

PONDER

1. What do you find most amazing about God's sovereignty as described in Acts 17:24-27?
2. As you look back at your life, how have you seen God's hand in leading you to live in certain places and times for his glory?
3. What do you find most difficult about where you find yourself today? How might the Lord give you perseverance through this challenge?

Then I saw a new heaven and a new earth, for the
first heaven and the first earth had passed away, and
the sea was no more. And I saw the holy city, new
Jerusalem, coming down out of heaven from God,
prepared as a bride adorned for her husband.
And I heard a loud voice from the throne saying,
"Behold, the dwelling place of God is with man.
He will dwell with them, and they will be his people,
and God himself will be with them as their God.
He will wipe away every tear from their eyes,
and death shall be no more, neither shall there
be mourning, nor crying, nor pain anymore,
for the former things have passed away."

Revelation 21:1-4

Jesus's resurrection is the beginning of God's new
project not to snatch people away from earth to
heaven but to colonize earth with the life of heaven.

N. T. Wright

30

FIXER UPPER

THROUGHOUT THESE *30 DAYS OF EXILE*, we have looked at a collection of Bible passages that encourage us to live faithfully as Christian exiles in this world. On Day 11 of this study we considered what Hebrews 11:13-16 tells us regarding some of the earliest Old Testament saints who were themselves strangers and exiles on earth:

> *These all died in faith, not having received the things promised, but having seen them and greeted them from afar, and having acknowledged that they were strangers and exiles on the earth. For people who speak thus make it clear that they are seeking a homeland. If they had been thinking of that land from which they had gone out, they would have had opportunity to return. But as it is, they desire a better country, that is, a heavenly one. Therefore, God is not ashamed to be called their God, for he has prepared for them a city.*

They were seeking a "homeland," a "better country, that is, a heavenly one," and God is preparing for them "a city." That homeland/country for which all the saints in Christ wait is the new earth in which the new heavens dwell and that city which God prepares is the new Jerusalem. This is what we all long for. This is the true land from which we have been exiled because it is the dwelling place of God. This is the home we will have for all eternity.

If you've been alive since 2013 you are probably familiar with the television show *Fixer Upper* and its stars Chip and Joanna Gaines. In the show, the Gaines take a home that needs major renovation and over the course of a number of weeks, they and their team of contractors transform an unremarkable space to a place of domestic beauty. As the homeowners are brought to their newly renovated home, there is a big unveiling in the final minutes of the show that often results in tears, hugs, high fives, and expressions of utter joy. For these residents, this space where they will spend so much time is now filled with more loveliness than they could have imagined.

Friends, what awaits us in our soon-to-be, perfectly transformed, God-inhabited home on the new earth is beyond comparison or analogy. I want you to think about the place of greatest physical beauty that you've ever visited. For me, it is Lucerne, Switzerland (just go to Google Images to see). However, Lucerne doesn't scratch the surface of the grandeur of our heavenly home when this black-and-white world is forever changed into 4K OLED quality color. Now, think about the time in which you most felt the warmth of God's presence. For me, there have been seasons of private prayer and worship that were truly life-transforming. But even those experiences do not come close to what life in heaven will be like when we talk to Jesus face-to-face and he walks beside us along mountainside paths and through streets of cities filled with righteousness.

In some respects, this passage of Scripture should have been placed on Day 1, for this is the greatest vision of what life is meant to be and what life will be for those who are found in Christ. However, I've left it here on the last day of this devotional study of our exile because I want it to be the perspective you keep with you. The promise that these "former things will pass away" ought to give us hope and confidence to live for Christ and his kingdom today (Revelation 21:4). In light of these realities to come, we should boldly set the GPS of our life toward those things that will not pass away – unseen, eternal, gospel-driven purposes that lead people to experience that for which we long.

PRAYER

Father, set my heart on heaven – on the new heavens and new earth – that will be my home when you make all things new. Help me to live with this "better country" as the place in which I find my greatest identity. Make me an ambassador of this land and its King, that I may invite all I can to join me in the greatest of human experiences – knowing and walking with you, my Creator and Savior. Amen.

PONDER

1. Which truth about God from Revelation 21:1-4 most encourages you?
2. What are you most longing for in your heavenly home?
3. What changes do you need to make today that would lead you to live more for those things that will last and less for those things that will pass away?

Conclusion
LIONS AND TIGERS AND BEARS, OH MY!

A T ONE POINT IN *THE WIZARD OF OZ*, Dorothy, the Tin Man, and the Scarecrow find themselves walking a portion of the yellow brick road through a dark forest. As they inch deeper and deeper into the forest, their thoughts of what lurks behind the next bend begin to create heightened levels of anxiety in their hearts. "Lions and tigers and bears" are all they can think about – dangerous creatures that would surely devour them. As you may remember, they do come into contact with one of these deadly animals, a lion. Though fearsome at first glance, when Dorothy stands up to him, the lion reveals his true nature to be one filled with cowardice.

As you and I walk this portion of our own yellow brick road, it's easy for us to also find ourselves saying the same thing: "lions and tigers and bears, oh my!" We start looking around at the challenges we presently face as Christians in the West and wonder what's around the bend – what danger might be lurking just ahead. Most of the time "the lion" never appears, or even when he does, he shows himself to be far weaker than we imagined.

I don't mean to minimize what has been rapidly occurring in our culture over the past couple of decades—the erosion of truth, the rejection of biblical sexual ethics, the growing hostility toward Christians (evangelicals in particular), increasing racial division, and deepening political tribalism (with Marxism at one extreme and nationalism at the other). No, I take each of these issues quite seriously. I also don't pretend these issues couldn't get worse and ultimately lead to scenarios that make living for Christ far more difficult. It's simply that I have come to realize two things regarding these present and potential difficulties: 1) that if I put too much of my focus upon the "lions and tigers and bears," then my heart easily weighs me down and I find myself getting angry or scared, and 2) that those Christians who have lost everything for Christ would tell me that he is worth it and that our God is faithful.

So, with that being the case, here is my prayer for you and me: that the Lord would give us a radical, supernatural reorientation of how we view our lives in this world. We would truly fix our minds upon unseen, eternal realities that are right here among us (2 Corinthians 4). We would turn often to our loving, omnipresent Father who delights in our voice (Psalm 46). We would live in the power of the Spirit of Christ who abides in us (2 Timothy 1). We would pray through the prism of the ongoing cosmic conflict between spiritual forces of good and evil – "your kingdom come" and "deliver us from evil" (Ephesians 6; Matthew 6). We would begin to see that life with the veil torn away looks far more like *The Lord of the Rings* than we could ever imagine (2 Kings 6). We would choose to center our identity in this world on the fact that we are redeemed, regenerated image-bearers of God who have been granted status as co-heirs with Christ of a kingdom that will soon descend upon the earth (Romans 8). While we are here, we have been called to serve as ambassadors of the King, who has asked us to bring an appeal of reconciliation to the world (2 Corinthians 5).

May the Lord answer this prayer that our exile here on earth may be filled with greater peace and joy, and more importantly, that through our exile Jesus may be glorified among our neighbors and the nations.

Soli Deo Gloria!

The mission of Central Bible Church is "Making God known by making disciples who are changed by God to change their world." We are a Kingdom-minded church committed to training leaders and laypeople through the surrender of all our resources. Your purchase of this book provides spiritual growth resources like this to others who are unable to afford them. If you believe this book would encourage your spiritual walk, but cannot afford it, we will gladly give you a copy.

To request discounts on bulk copies or to make a contribution to our local and global leadership training, please contact us:

centralpress@wearecentral.org.

Learn more about the ministry of Central Bible Church online at www.wearecentral.org.

Central Bible Church
8001 Anderson Boulevard
Fort Worth, Texas 76120
817-274-1315

Made in the USA
Coppell, TX
26 August 2021

61259468R00083